New Directions for
Adult and Continuing
Education

Susan Imel
Jovita M. Ross-Gordon
COEDITORS-IN-CHIEF

Teaching Strategies in the Online Environment

Simone C. O. Conceição

EDITOR

Number 113 • Spring 2(
Jossey-Bass
San Francisco

TEACHING STRATEGIES AND IMPLICATIONS FOR ONLINE AND ADULT EDUCATION
Simone C.O. Conceição (ed.)
New Directions for Adult and Continuing Education, no. 113
Susan Imel, Jovita M. Ross-Gordon, Coeditors-in-Chief

Microfilm copies of issues and articles are available in 16mm and 35mm, as well as microfiche in 105mm, through University Microfilms Inc., 300 North Zeeb Road, Ann Arbor, Michigan 48106-1346.

NEW DIRECTIONS FOR ADULT AND CONTINUING EDUCATION (ISSN 1052-2891, electronic ISSN 1536-0717) is part of The Jossey-Bass Higher and Adult Education Series and is published quarterly by Wiley Subscription Services, Inc., A Wiley Company, at Jossey-Bass, 989 Market Street, San Francisco, California 94103-1741. Periodicals Postage Paid at San Francisco, California, and at additional mailing offices. POSTMASTER: Send address changes to New Directions for Adult and Continuing Education, Jossey-Bass, 989 Market Street, San Francisco, California 94103-1741.

SUBSCRIPTIONS cost $80.00 for individuals and $195.00 for institutions, agencies, and libraries.

EDITORIAL CORRESPONDENCE should be sent to the Coeditors-in-Chief, Susan Imel, ERIC/ACVE, 1900 Kenny Road, Columbus, Ohio 43210-1090, e-mail: imel.l@osu.edu; or Jovita M. Ross-Gordon, Southwest Texas State University, EAPS Dept., 601 University Drive, San Marcos, TX 78666.

Cover photograph by Jack Hollingsworth@Photodisc

Wiley Bicentennial Logo: Richard J. Pacifico

www.josseybass.com

CONTENTS

EDITOR'S NOTES

The past few years have witnessed rapid changes in the field of adult and continuing education associated with the increased use of distance education technologies to deliver online education. The proliferation of online education has allowed better access, convenience, and flexibility as a way to support adult learners' educational opportunities. Eastmond (1998) says that the use of online instruction has held "important educational promise for engendering active and experiential learning, encouraging reflection and application, and fostering collaboration and individualized construction of meaning in learning communities" (p. 40). Online courses call for reflection on how new information and experiences relate to the context of learners' prior knowledge and how discussions in an online environment allow learners to collaborate.

Moreover, online teaching has changed the way adult educators interact with learners by challenging the traditional social structure of teaching. The role of the instructor has changed from "sage on the stage" and is replaced in practice by the "guide on the side" (Baldwin, 1998). This new concept moves the instructor away from being the source of authority and knowledge (McDonald and Postle, 1999) to being an individual who plays a supportive role as individuals learn (Gillespie, 1998). Therefore, the traditional concept of teaching and learning is questioned in the online environment. For some practitioners, teaching and learning becomes a partnership. The instructor provides leadership, designs the environment, and manages the process; the learner engages the environment, collaborating with other learners and experts to construct knowledge (Doherty, 1998). Learning becomes an active, constructive process in which learners strategically manage cognitive resources to create new knowledge.

One of the challenges for adult educators who teach online is to identify teaching strategies that fit the needs of learners, content, and the environment. This volume describes a variety of teaching strategies, research on the use of these teaching strategies in the online environment, examples of how these teaching strategies have been used in online courses, a consideration of the effectiveness and limitations of these strategies, and implications for the practice of adult and continuing education.

This volume contains nine chapters. Chapter One provides guidelines for understanding the online environment and the use of online teaching strategies. In Chapter Two, Garnet Grosjean and Thomas Sork devote significant attention to the administrative challenges of setting up two online experiences, particularly with regard to the international case study. They

address how administrative and infrastructure concerns are essential to the success of online teaching, or more specifically to the success of moving face-to-face courses to the online environment.

Chapters Three to Eight focus on six teaching strategies for the online environment: using consensus groups, concept mapping, holistic mentoring, knowledge repositories, online discussion boards, and online assessment and evaluation. In Chapter Three, Regina Smith and John Dirkx describe the use of online consensus group work, a form of collaborative learning. Cooperative learning, which is differentiated from collaborative learning, involves individual effort, but students work together in small groups to address well-defined and well-structured problems and questions. In this situation, the overall focus is on mastery of a body of knowledge. In group work, the learner must acknowledge dissent and disagreement and cope with difference and ambiguity.

Chapter Four presents the use of concept maps, a cognitive learning strategy that promotes meaningful learning. Barbara Daley, Alberto Cañas, and Tracy Stark-Schweitzer examine the use of concept maps in online environments through a discussion of CmapTools software as a teaching, learning, and evaluation strategy. They highlight the research base supporting concept maps and use practical examples to illustrate the effectiveness of these maps in online courses.

Chapter Five focuses on facilitators as mentors in online education, essentially attending to the whole student in providing support, challenge, and vision for their clientele. Kimberly Burgess provides a review of the literature on online counseling and mentoring as a framework and concludes with an explanation of how facilitators can incorporate these mentoring models into their practice.

In Chapter Six, Rosemary Lehman explains how educational institutions around the world are in the process of transformation from centers of compartmentalized and departmentalized knowledge development to communities of knowledge sharing. To enable this sharing, digital knowledge repositories are being created. This chapter looks at the growing interest in digital knowledge repositories, their evolving nature, and the accepted specifications (standards) for encoding objects of knowledge (commonly called learning objects) for mutual retrieval and collaboration.

Chapter Seven addresses the use of discussion boards based on the assumption that they provide a unique potential that is not automatically present in face-to-face learning situations. S. Joseph Levine explains that discussion boards have the unique capacity to support higher-order constructivist learning and the development of a learning community.

Chapter Eight discusses assessment and evaluation of students in the online environment, including the use of different forms of rubrics. Stevie Rocco focuses on two forms of measurement: those that assess the learner during the course of a unit or lesson and those that judge whether a student has met the objectives of the unit or lesson on completing the lesson.

New Directions for Adult and Continuing Education • DOI: 10.1002/ace

Chapter Nine summarizes and synthesizes the major emphases from the various chapters, examining their practical implications, and suggesting future directions for adult and continuing education.

This volume offers suggestions for the effective use of teaching strategies in the online environment. Practitioners and novices will find it valuable as a basis for identifying sound teaching practices and a guide for making efficient and caring instructional decisions.

Finally, I thank Luciana Ugrina for helping me edit this volume.

Simone C. O. Conceição
Editor

References

Baldwin, R. G. "Technology's Impact on Faculty Life and Work." In K. H. Gillespie (ed.), *The Impact of Technology on Faculty Development, Life, and Work*. New Directions for Teaching and Learning, no. 76. San Francisco: Jossey-Bass, 1998.

Doherty, P. B. "Learner Control in Asynchronous Learning Environments." ALN Magazine, 1998, 2(2). Retrieved Dec 27, 2006, from http://www.sloan-c.org/publications/magazine/v2n2/doherty.asp.

Eastmond, D. V. "Adult Learners and Internet-Based Distance Education." In B. Cahoon (ed.), *Adult Learning and the Internet*. New Directions for Adult and Continuing Education, no. 78. San Francisco: Jossey-Bass, 1998.

Gillespie, K. H. "Instructional Design for the New Technologies." In K. H. Gillespie (ed.), *The Impact of Technology on Faculty Development, Life, and Work*. New Directions for Teaching and Learning, no. 76. San Francisco: Jossey-Bass, 1998.

McDonald, J., and Postle, G. "Teaching Online: Challenge to a Reinterpretation of Traditional Instructional Models." Paper presented at the Fifth Australian World Wide Web Conference, Southern Cross University, Toowoomba, Queensland, Mar. 3, 1999. Retrieved Dec. 26, 2006, from http://www.usq.edu.au/users/mcdonalj/papers/paper.htm.

SIMONE C.O. CONCEIÇÃO is an assistant professor of adult and continuing education at the University of Wisconsin-Milwaukee.

1

This chapter provides guidelines for understanding the online environment and the use of online teaching strategies.

Understanding the Environment for Online Teaching

Simone C. O. Conceição

As adult educators begin online teaching, a number of concerns have emerged. There is no doubt that teaching online is different from teaching face-to-face, and the characteristics of online learners are different from more traditional classroom students. Many online learners are adults for whom attending class at a campus facility is not easy because of their life situations. Some who pursue online learning are midcareer professionals seeking continuing education. Nonetheless the audience for online education is growing quickly, and the makeup of online learners is changing.

Teaching online requires a considerable amount of time to design, develop, and deliver a course. In the online environment, even more than in the face-to-face environment, it is critical that the educator move beyond traditional notions of the instructor as conveyor of information to embody the role long espoused in adult education literature of instructor as facilitator. The instructor must gain comfort and proficiency in using the Web as the primary instructor-learner connection in order to teach effectively without visual and verbal cues.

Teaching effectively online requires an understanding of the benefits and limitations of the Web as a teaching and learning tool. An online course is not simply a traditional course translated into a Web language. The instructor needs to rethink the learner role, the teacher role, and the design of instruction in this new environment. Thus, a focus on the design that includes effective teaching strategies is essential.

NEW DIRECTIONS FOR ADULT AND CONTINUING EDUCATION, no. 113, Spring 2007 © 2007 Wiley Periodicals, Inc.
Published online in Wiley InterScience (www.interscience.wiley.com) • DOI: 10.1002/ace.242

This volume is based on the premise that online teaching requires careful planning of instructional strategies. There is a wide variety of teaching strategies available for supporting online learning. This chapter provides guidelines for understanding the online environment and the use of online teaching strategies based on research, with a focus on online learner characteristics, the role of the online instructor, and guiding principles for effective online instruction.

Online Learners

Understanding learner characteristics is essential for designing online instruction. The learner is the most important element of the online learning environment and should be considered early in the design and implementation of the online learning experience. The more an instructor understands online learners, the better the experience will be for everyone (Moore and Kearsley, 1996).

Adult learners of any age, educational level, and educational needs are pursuing adult and continuing education in an online format. A common characteristic of these learners is their commitment to education. Moreover, they tend to be independent self-starters and highly motivated (Simonson, Smaldino, Albright, and Zvacek, 2006).

There are some important skills learners should have in order to have a successful online learning experience. Among them are basic computer skills and access to a working computer and Internet connection; time management, including having a routine schedule to participate in the course; the ability to devote at least ten hours a week for each three-credit course; the ability to work both independently and in teams; the discipline to complete assignments by deadlines rather than waiting until the end of the course; motivation to read, write, and participate in class activities; flexibility to deal with technology issues; and the ability to ask questions to clarify an issue in the class.

Role of the Online Instructor

Online instructors may take on a variety of roles depending on the tasks performed during the design and delivery of the online course and influenced by learner characteristics, content, and course environment. These roles are described in different ways. Conceição (2006) characterizes the successful online instructor as an instructional designer, facilitator, catalyst, and learner. During the development phase of the course, the instructor takes on the role of an instructional designer—an individual who designs, organizes, administers, and presents course content. During the course delivery, the instructor takes on the role of facilitator, catalyst, and learner. In the role of a facilitator, a person who moves from the center of instruction to the sidelines, the instructor engages learners in the learning process. As a catalyst, the instructor instigates conversations. And as a learner, the instructor participates and learns with others in the online environment.

Coppola, Hiltz, and Rotter (2001) identified three roles for the online instructor based on tasks performed during the delivery of the course: cognitive, affective, and managerial. Roles that are cognitive in nature are linked to the mental processes of learning, information storage, and thinking. The affective role stems from the relationships of students, instructor, and the classroom environment. The managerial role is associated with class and course management. Coppola, Hiltz, and Rotter characterize these roles as a change in the "teaching persona" (p. 9) that occurs as the result of the formality of communication and lack of spontaneity when communicating with learners. The formality of communication occurs when instructions given to students are precise. Although the teaching process is described as formal, instructors find their relationship with learners more intimate in the online environment.

Anderson, Rourke, Garrison, and Archer (2001) use a framework to describe the context of instruction based on a model of critical thinking and practical inquiry. Their model considers three components of teaching and learning in a text-based environment: cognitive presence, social presence, and teaching presence. Out of this model, three instructor roles emerged: designer of the educational experience, facilitator and co-creator of a social environment, and subject matter expert. Under this model, teaching presence involves design and administration, discourse facilitation, and direct instruction. Design and administration involve precision and transparency in planning instruction. Discourse facilitation involves cognitive and affective effort on the part of the instructor to maintain the interest, motivation, and engagement of learners in active learning. Direct instruction focuses on intellectual and scholarly leadership by sharing subject matter knowledge with learners. In this model, the instructor sets the climate of the class and models the qualities of a scholar; both roles require cognitive and affective effort.

Tasks related to the delivery of the course involve some type of interaction among students, content, and technology. According to Coppola, Hiltz, and Rotter (2002), these tasks are categorized as cognitive, affective, and managerial. Cognitive tasks include responding to questions; editing questions and responses to questions; thinking, reasoning, and analyzing information; and helping students engage in rehearsing and retrieving information. Affective tasks comprise behavior related to influencing students' relationships with the instructor and with other students and the virtual classroom environment. Managerial tasks during the delivery of the course include getting students into the conference as well as interactions with other support staff, motivating and coordinating students to participate in the course, and monitoring and evaluating student learning outcomes.

Other tasks that Anderson, Rourke, Garrison, and Archer (2001) employed during the delivery of the course include facilitating discourse, which means regularly reading and commenting on student postings; establishing and maintaining the discourse that creates and sustains social presence; encouraging, acknowledging, or reinforcing student contributions; setting the climate for learning; sharing responsibility with each student for attaining agreed-on learning objectives; supporting and encouraging student responses; drawing in less active participants; and assessing the efficacy of the process.

Anderson, Rourke, Garrison, and Archer (2001) describe direct instruction as one of the instructor tasks. It consists of presenting content and questions; focusing the discussion on specific issues; summarizing the discussion; confirming understanding through assessment and explanatory feedback; diagnosing misconceptions; injecting knowledge from diverse sources, such as textbooks, articles, the Internet, and personal experience; and responding to technical concerns. The direct instruction tasks include functions similar to what Coppola, Hiltz, and Rotter (2001) describe as cognitive or affective tasks.

The role of the online instructor is one of support in the teaching-learning process and is characterized by new tasks. Teaching and learning become a partnership resulting from the learner-centered environment. These environments are not controllable and predictable; they require instructors to think about themselves very differently than they did in the past, recognize the changes in the educational paradigm, engage in new kinds of activities, and reconsider the meaning of being an expert.

Guiding Principles for Effective Online Instruction

Successful online teaching depends on the design and facilitation of instruction through the use of effective teaching strategies, including some strategies that are appropriate for any teaching-learning environment and some that are particularly critical in the online teaching environment. Graham and others (2001) offer a set of guiding principles for effective online teaching based on the Seven Principles for Good Practice in Undergraduate Education (Chickering and Gamson, 1987).

Principle 1: Good Practice Encourages Student-Faculty Contact
- Instructors should provide clear guidelines for interaction with learners that describe the types of communication addressed in the online course. For example, the instructor may use discussion forums for clarifying issues and student socialization. It is imperative that the instructor explain the purpose of communication to help students understand the interaction process.

- Instructors should determine a standard for time lines to respond to messages and let students know what the standards are.

Principle 2: Good Practice Encourages Cooperation Among Students

- Instructors should create well-designed discussion assignments with guidelines for participation in asynchronous discussion that encourage meaningful learning. Participation in online discussion should be considered a requirement, and learners' grades should depend on participation.
- Discussion groups should be small, limited to five to seven students per group.
- Online discussions should focus on a specific task that will result in an outcome or product produced by the group. Tasks should be motivating and engage learners in the content.
- Instructors should provide feedback to learners on their discussion participation. Evaluation of participation should be based on the quality of their postings. Expectations for the online discussions should be available for learners from the start of the course.

Principle 3: Good Practice Encourages Active Learning

- Instructors should use a variety of teaching strategies that encourage active learning and group work such as case studies, problem-based scenarios, or creation of a program.
- Instructors should provide opportunities for learners to obtain valuable skills by presenting their projects and performing at a higher level through seeing and discussing their peers' work.
- Instructors should use synchronous or asynchronous interactions among students to allow them to share and discuss projects.

Principle 4: Good Practice Gives Prompt Feedback

- Instructors should provide information feedback when answering to a question or grading an assignment and providing comments.
- Instructors should provide acknowledgment feedback to confirm that some event has occurred. This type of feedback acknowledges the receipt of an assignment or an e-mail from a student asking a specific question. An instructor may send an e-mail note acknowledging it and informing that the message will be answered soon.
- Instructors should provide detailed personal feedback to each learner. If time does not permit giving prompt feedback to individual students, responding to the whole class may be sufficient. A class message can address patterns and trends in the discussion without being overwhelmed by the amount of feedback to be given.

Principle 5: Good Practice Emphasizes Time on Task

- Instructors should provide course deadlines to encourage learners to spend time on tasks and avoid procrastination. Deadlines also provide a context for regular contact with the instructor and other students.

Principle 6: Good Practice Communicates High Expectations
- Instructors should communicate high expectations for learner performance by giving challenging assignments. Assigning tasks that require students to apply theories to real-life situations rather than recalling facts or concepts is essential. One way to address this principle is to have learners work on a case-based approach that involves real-life issues with authentic data gathered from actual situations.
- Instructors should provide examples for learners to model, along with comments explaining why the examples are good.
- Instructors should publicly praise exemplary work to communicate high expectations. One way to accomplish this is to call attention to insightful or well-presented student postings.

Principle 7: Good Practice Respects Diverse Talents and Ways of Learning
- Instructors should provide opportunities for learners to be creative with their own course work by selecting project topics according to established guidelines. Allowing learners to research their own topics of interest and encouraging them to express their own points of view incorporates diverse views into online courses.
- Instructors should provide guidelines to assist learners in selecting their topics relevant to the course and still allow them to share their unique perspectives with the rest of the class.

Based on the guiding principles for effective online teaching in a learner-centered environment, instructors may use online teaching strategies that enable learners to share in the process of selecting and developing content. A continuum may exist as to the level of focus on the learner. At one end of the continuum, the instructor may be a fully participating member of the group, with no unalterable assumptions about the content or direction of the course, or both content to be covered and teaching strategies are negotiated with the group (Hanna, Glowacki-Dudka, and Conceição-Runlee, 2000).

In an interactive online course, the instructor may want to provide a framework for the course with flexibility and opportunity for negotiation of the content and format. Since an online environment requires prior preparation of the course, it is useful to have such a framework for the course already designed. The instructor then facilitates the class through discussion and problem-posing dialogue, referring to external resources as needed. The instructor may balance his or her role as a member of the learning group but also as a facilitator and expert when called on to work in this capacity (Hanna, Glowacki-Dudka, and Conceição-Runlee, 2000).

A variety of online teaching strategies can be used to provide meaningful experiences to online learners. Adult learners have different styles of learning, but in the online environment, there is no difference. Thus, an instructor who is designing online instruction may want to use multiple teaching strategies to meet diverse learners' needs.

New Directions for Adult and Continuing Education • DOI: 10.1002/ace

These are just a few examples of how the guiding principles may be used. These principles can serve as a framework for novice adult educators who are embarking on online teaching or as a refresher for experienced online instructors.

Subsequent chapters in this volume focus on teaching strategies that have been successfully used in the online environment and are based on the guiding principles for effective online instruction. The strategies examined are online consensus groups, concept maps, holistic mentoring, learning object repositories, discussion boards, and evaluation and assessment strategies.

References

Anderson, T., Rourke, L., Garrison, D. R., and Archer, W. "Assessing Teaching Presence in a Computer Conferencing Context." Journal of Asynchronous Learning Networks, 2001, 5(2), 1–17. Retrieved June 19, 2006, from http://www.aln.org/alnweb/journal/jaln-vol5issue2v2.htm.

Chickering, A., and Gamson, Z. "Seven Principles of Good Practice in Undergraduate Education." *AAHE Bulletin,* 1987, 39, 3–7.

Conceição, S.C.O. "Faculty Lived Experiences in the Online Environment." *Adult Education Quarterly,* 2006, 57(1), 1–20.

Coppola, N. W., Hiltz, S. R., and Rotter, N. "Becoming a Virtual Professor: Pedagogical Roles and Asynchronous Learning Networks." *Journal of Management Information Systems,* 2002, 18, 169–190.

Graham, C., and others. "Seven Principles of Effective Teaching: A Practical Lens for Evaluating Online Courses." Technology Source Archives, Apr. 2001. Retrieved Oct. 14, 2006, from http://technologysource.org/article/seven_principles_of_effective_teaching/.

Hanna, D., Glowacki-Dudka, M., and Conceição-Runlee, S. *147 Practical Tips for Teaching Online Groups: Essentials of Web-Based Education.* Madison, Wis.: Atwood Publishing, 2000.

Moore, M. G., and Kearsley, G. *Distance Education: A Systems View.* (2nd ed.) Belmont, Calif.: Thomson-Wadsworth, 1996.

Simonson, M., Smaldino, S., Albright, M., and Zvacek, S. *Teaching and Learning at a Distance: Foundations of Distance Education.* (3rd ed.) Upper Saddle River, N.J.: Pearson-Merrill/Prentice Hall, 2006.

SIMONE C.O. CONCEIÇÃO is an assistant professor of adult and continuing education at the University of Wisconsin-Milwaukee.

2

This chapter discusses two case studies where face-to-face courses were converted into online courses.

Going Online: Uploading Learning to the Virtual Classroom

Garnet Grosjean, Thomas J. Sork

The rapidly increasing number of Web-based courses and degrees has sparked renewed interest in distance education. Educational institutions and private companies are moving to online delivery. The number and variety of Web-based courses and programs is escalating at a frenetic pace as providers compete to capture market share. Marketing of online learning is carefully framed as delivering educational opportunities to students at locations and times of their convenience, enabling them to cultivate responsibility for their own learning. In fact, offering online courses may be a crucial factor in the survival of modern educational institutions. But as the number of online courses increases, the challenges in their development and delivery become more apparent. Initially, universities simply repackaged face-to-face course materials and posted them to a Web site. But as demand increased, the approaches to online course development became more sophisticated, and a set of best practices emerged to guide the design and delivery of online education.

Planning Courses for Online Delivery

Currently courses are crafted for online delivery in two distinct ways: new courses are developed to meet a specific need, or existing courses are converted to an online format. In this chapter we focus on the second option, the conversion of existing courses for delivery in online programs, and address the underlying theory. It is important that the process be user driven, not technology driven. Technology provides the tools that allow users (students) to address the tasks set by the program.

NEW DIRECTIONS FOR ADULT AND CONTINUING EDUCATION, no. 113, Spring 2007 © 2007 Wiley Periodicals, Inc.
Published online in Wiley InterScience (www.interscience.wiley.com) • DOI: 10.1002/ace.243

Issues in Converting Face-to-Face Courses

The goal in converting an existing face-to-face course to an online format is to ensure a quality user experience. Thus, developmental issues must be carefully thought through. A primary concern is maintaining the pedagogical integrity of the course in the translation from traditional face-to-face delivery. Another issue is whether to adopt a team approach or whether a single instructor should develop the course. This decision involves identifying who should be involved in the process, when they should be involved, and why they should be involved. Furthermore, faculty members who participate in the delivery of the online course must be able to acquire the skills and competencies required to teach online.

Establishing realistic time lines is an important step in the conversion of any face-to-face course to online delivery; the introduction of technology often requires additional training or support and may extend development time. Time lines also vary depending on whether the course is offered for credit, given at the graduate or undergraduate level, or offered locally or internationally.

Challenges. Beyond the technical and theoretical challenges in developing a course for online delivery, difficulties should be anticipated in recruiting appropriate faculty as online instructors. Not every classroom instructor is capable of making the transition from the brick-and-mortar classroom to the virtual classroom. And not every faculty member wishes to participate in online development or instruction. The recruitment of appropriate faculty has been likened to a courtship ritual, because faculty require incentives to undertake the additional work load that comes with online instruction. The extra commitment is significant. First, faculty must learn the technological aspects of teaching online. Second, they need to accommodate the additional time required to respond to students' queries in textual rather than verbal format. Third, they must recognize the complexities of teaching students from different countries and different cultural contexts.

Evaluation in the Virtual Classroom. Evaluating online courses is problematic in a number of ways. Student evaluations at the end of a face-to-face course traditionally focus on their experience with a particular instructor. In online education, however, the instructor's role is only one part of a much broader experience. The technology, the user interface, and the design of content are all keys in understanding the online learner's experience. Such a broad spectrum of factors demands new methods to evaluate the learner's experience in an online course. For example, the visual cues traditionally available in face-to-face instruction are almost completely absent in the virtual classroom, requiring online instructors to identify and use different cues—for example, student participation in discussions and small group work or tracking student movements around the Web site.

In the rest of this chapter we discuss two cases in which face-to-face courses were converted into online formats: a course in a collaborative master of education program in adult learning and global change involving four universities on four continents, and conversion of a face-to-face diploma-level course in planning, first to traditional correspondence delivery and subsequently to online format.

Case 1: Adult Learning and Global Change

This case describes the process and procedures used in converting a traditional graduate course (Work and Education) to an online course (Work and Learning) for delivery in the adult learning and global change master of education (ALGC) program at the University of British Columbia. We used a collaborative process to determine the need for the course and developed a plan for curriculum conversion. The conversion involved analysis of the curriculum to determine the appropriate process, development of online course materials, and implementation of the revised curriculum.

A large and rapidly increasing body of literature is available to anyone interested in learning how to develop courses for online delivery. For example, a simple Google search returns more than twenty-four thousand hits in response to the search phrase "developing online courses." A sizable literature also exists on academy-industry cooperation in the design and delivery of online courses. But multiuniversity collaborations in the development and delivery of a graduate degree in adult education of the type described here are rare; there are few published examples. The story of the development and delivery of the ALGC is one of a radically different master of education program (Abrandt Dahlgren, Larsson, and Walters, 2006; Larsson and others, 2005). Accounts of this program focus on the nature of the cooperative process that joined four universities on four continents in the program's development and delivery: University of British Columbia (UBC), Canada; University of Technology (UTS), Australia; Linköping University (LiU), Sweden; and University of the Western Cape (UWC), South Africa. Our account focuses on the process and challenges in converting a traditional (classroom-based, face-to-face, on-campus) course to one appropriate for online, intercontinental delivery.

Development of the ALGC Program. Development of the ALGC program required extensive negotiation of content and delivery methods among the four universities. Planning began in 1998, and the first students were admitted in 2001. The program offers global perspectives on learning in cross-cultural environments. Faculty at each of the partner universities develop and deliver individual courses in which students collaborate across countries, using resources from the different settings in which they are located. Each of the four partner universities admits students, ensuring a complex four-continent cohort.

New Directions for Adult and Continuing Education • DOI: 10.1002/ace

Converting a traditional course for online delivery is not a simple or linear process. A number of challenges must be overcome, some of which require skills in the use of technology. The challenges increase almost exponentially when conversion is attempted within the context of an intercontinental partnership. The four partner institutions first determined that six core courses would be required to cover the program's content, and then they identified which university was best equipped to develop which course. Each institution was responsible for the faculty and staff resources needed to develop their assigned courses. The standard format adopted required sections on (1) aims and objectives, (2) content, (3) modes of delivery, (4) activity requirements, and (5) assessment. An additional consideration, related to the process of having the program approved by each university, set up additional barriers to program implementation. UBC was chosen to develop a course on the changing relationship of the economy, workplace learning, and adult education. The development process is described below.

Aims and Objectives. Our first decision was whether to create a new online graduate course or convert an existing face-to-face course to online format. Expediency, combined with a lack of resources, contributed to the decision to convert an existing course, Work and Education, currently offered on-campus, to Work and Learning, to be offered online. In reviewing our aims and objectives, it soon became clear that the purpose of the course would have to be recast in a global perspective to accommodate the geographical distribution of students. To do so we combined international research traditions from adult education, the sociology of work, labor studies, organizational theory, and economics with localized experience to be derived from course participants. Two key themes prevailed: (1) the changing discourse on work and learning and (2) workplace learning.

In the conversion process, we almost overlooked an important consideration. To that point, the purpose and objectives of the course had been framed within a teaching-learning perspective. We soon realized, however, that the framing would have to change to recognize the different cultural contexts of the other institutional partners and their students. So to geographical considerations we had to add cultural considerations, both institutional and individual.

When considering the cross-cultural complexities of teaching and learning processes in the countries developing the program, we had to address the diverse needs of students who may be studying in a different culture and in a language that is not their first language. The decision to conduct the program using English forced us to recognize that the ability to assign meanings to concepts and discussions would require translation in many cases, and this created its own constraints and power structures.

The language of delivery was only one of the concerns when considering the delivery of courses to culturally diverse groups of students. There were a number of additional considerations: cultural differences, religious and social class differences and interactions, learning style differences, and prejudices and predetermined expectations. This resulted in the integration of international comparisons and examples into the curriculum while being careful to include information on Netiquette—the appropriate etiquette for Internet-based communications and methods of appropriate feedback—to address issues of respect, equity, and fairness in dealing with participants in the program as a reciprocal endeavor. This was based on the understanding that in cross-cultural situations, participants would continually be dealing with socially differentiated ways of understanding and that faculty teaching in the program would have to interact with cultural sensitivity with the students while simultaneously sensitizing students to issues of difference and equity.

Beyond the discussions of cross-cultural complexities among the partners developing the program, invaluable assistance was provided by requesting feedback on course content and methods of delivery from international students enrolled in on-campus courses at our university. What was not considered at the time, however, was the possibility that some students would suffer from disruption caused by political upheaval or natural disasters in certain parts of the world.

Content. Once the purpose and themes of the course were established, we began to consider content and staging in relation to the order of courses the cohort would move through. Work and Learning would be the third of six core courses. It would follow Adult Learning and precede Fostering Learning in Practice. The content of Work and Learning would have to build on the former and provide an introduction to the latter. To accomplish this, we divided the course content into two blocks. The first would address the changing nature of work; the second would relate to workforce education and training.

In block one, we chose to depart from the critical analysis of the local labor market that characterized our on-campus course. We expanded the content to make visible shifts in paid and unpaid work, the changing structure of labor markets, and the effects of such shifts on different societal groups. This approach would provide students with an overview of how the discourse on work and learning is changing and was portrayed in various national policy debates. The course then examined the debate on employability skills and explored the link between work organization, labor processes, and skill formation. Finally, we introduced the consequences of economic democracy as an alternative approach to the skills debate.

In block two, we examined the concept of the learning organization to see what practices could be learned from theory and what theory could be learned from practice. Building on the first core course on adult learning, we discussed the impact of work processes and work organization on workplace learning. The course was designed to encourage investigation of why employers chose or declined to invest in employee training and reviewed different forms of workplace learning. With this approach, we would provide students with an introduction to learning in practice, in preparation for the Fostering Learning in Practice course that immediately follows.

Modes of Delivery. In the ALGC program development process, we set the goal of making all syllabi, outlines, lectures, calendars, and assignments available online and ensuring that courses were uniform in appearance and navigation. Consistency in course format was a key factor in ensuring ease of navigation for students. This part of the conversion from classroom to online proved particularly challenging for us. The face-to-face components of the Work and Education course such as classroom discussions, small group work, and presentations had to be translated into an acceptable online alternative. After a lengthy review process, we chose the Blackboard Learning System as our Web site host. The discussion boards on Blackboard would help to replace the classroom discussions that are an essential part of face-to-face learning.

A number of steps had to be taken to prepare course material for use in an online environment. Documents had to be converted into HTML and PDF formats, and templates had to be created for the course on Blackboard (including the home page, course materials, reading lists, and assignment schedules). Another task required the uploading and linking of files to the appropriate sites on Blackboard in accordance with our agreement to ensure that all courses were uniform in appearance and navigation. We had to learn how to add and remove students from the courses, how to administer evaluation surveys on completion of the course, and how to collect and compile survey results. These tasks required a different set of skills and abilities from those required to develop the aims, objectives, and content of the course.

Since the Work and Learning course emphasizes differential understandings of the literature, the instructional format was designed to be as participatory as the distributed learning mode allowed. There would be assigned readings and textbooks, and, where appropriate, copies of readings and articles would be placed on the Web site in easily downloadable files. At this stage of course development, the challenging issue of copyright compliance had to be met. Because the four countries participating in the program had different intellectual property regimes, the partners resolved that the institution developing and delivering the course would take responsibility for compliance with legislation in their respective jurisdictions. When selecting material to post on the Blackboard site for the Work and Learning course, therefore, we had to ensure we met Canadian copyright requirements.

Activity Requirements. Students would be required to participate actively in online discussions by engaging with others on ideas from the readings or grounded in practical experience. Each student would take responsibility for leading one online discussion. Students would also work together on group assignments and student papers related to issues and trends in adult education, and work and learning would be posted on the site and form the basis for further comparative analysis.

Assessment. When attempting to determine assessment criteria for the Work and Learning course, we were confronted by another structural impediment in the different systems for grading assignments and courses in use by the partners. Two institutions (LiU and UTS) applied a pass-fail system; the other two (UBC and UWC) used a graded system for assessment. All partners had to comply with the regulations of their own institutions. Adoption of a common instrument for conversion of grading provided a solution. The European Credit Transfer System (ECTS) is a scale in seven grades that enables students to transfer academic credits from one institution to another in Europe. The ECTS grading scale ranges from "excellent" to "fail," assessed on the basis of combinations of keywords and definitions. Each university would then convert the ECTS scale into their respective institution's grading scheme.

Additional Barriers. Before we could launch the ALGC program, finances and local decision making had to be addressed. Each of the four countries had different ways of funding university programs, varying from no tuition to full tuition and combinations of the two. For example, students in Sweden pay no tuition fees; funding is provided by the state for a specified number of study spaces. In Australia, master's programs are financed solely by tuition fees. In South Africa and Canada, university programs are financed by a mix of state funding and tuition fees. We were concerned that many students would enroll through Linköping because of the tuition-free policy. If so, this would require additional resources for Linköping and restrict the resources of the other universities that require tuition to either wholly or partially support these initiatives. The solution was for each institution to restrict admission to students from its own country.

In terms of local decision making, three further obstacles had to be overcome: (1) the academic determination of what comprises a master's degree, (2) the local approval process for new courses and programs, and (3) the nature of the approval process. A thesis was required by two of the partner universities, but a course-based master's degree was available at the other two. This difference led to a decision that the program options should have flexibility; a local options component was introduced that constituted 25 percent of the program. In that period, two universities would have their students complete a thesis; in the other two universities, students would complete elective courses to make up the credits equivalent to the master's thesis.

The second challenge was in drafting the text of the program and course descriptions in a way that allowed the administrations of each university to adopt them without negotiation. The program was to some extent shaped by this adaptation to local expectations and norms, including the content of curriculum outlines regarding how assessments and courses should be described and the details of reference material required.

The third challenge was in the complexity of the approval process at each of the partner universities. These varied from three levels of decision making in Sweden to eight levels in Canada. The internal decision-making process at UBC was so complicated and slow that the university did not have the required approvals in place in time to meet the program's planned implementation date in 2001. UBC faculty therefore had to contribute to course development and teaching in the first cohort without having any UBC students in the program. This situation was rectified by the second intake of students in 2002, but a valuable opportunity to receive feedback from local students was lost until the second year, and the resources that students would have provided in tuition were also forgone.

Summary. Converting a traditional course for online delivery is not a simple or linear process. In this case, we have described the process and procedures used in converting a traditional graduate course, Work and Education, to Work and Learning, an online course for delivery in the ALGC program. We used a collaborative process to determine the need for the course in the program and subsequently developed a plan for the curriculum conversion. The process involved analysis of the curriculum to determine the appropriate conversion process, development of online course materials, and implementation of the plan. In case 2, we provide an example of the conversion of a face-to-face planning course first to a traditional correspondence format and more recently to a Web-based delivery.

Case 2: Program Planning

Since it was originally conceived in the 1970s, the course in question has carried the title Planning Short Courses, Workshops and Seminars and was designed as one of several required courses in UBC's adult education diploma program. The program was developed primarily as practical preparation in the basics of adult education for those who already possessed an undergraduate degree but did not wish to enroll in a master's program. As suggested by the title, the course covered knowledge and skills useful when planning programs in a short-term format, including conferences, symposia, and similar intensive, concentrated, face-to-face learning experiences. In addition to meeting part of the core requirements for the diploma, the face-to-face version of this course attracted large numbers of students from nursing, business, and other professions and disciplines who wanted a practical elective. This course had a reputation of requiring a lot of reading and lengthy assignments but was also regarded by students as highly practical. As the course went through these two conversions, we wanted to retain the elements that seemed to make it so valuable to students.

New Directions for Adult and Continuing Education • DOI: 10.1002/ace

The history leading up to the development of the online version is important to understand because it influenced the decisions we made about how to take it online and what elements of the face-to-face and correspondence versions should be retained, albeit in an online environment. There are certainly potential benefits to developing an online course unrestrained by history and earlier curriculum decisions, but there were several reasons we did not want to start from scratch. First, we were operating under a general university policy that required all distance education versions of face-to-face courses to provide essentially the same learning experience, or at least produce equivalent learning outcomes. Second, the course seemed to be doing what we wanted it to and was generally well received by students, so we did not want to tinker too much with what seemed to be a successful design. Third, our primary motive for going online was to improve student access rather than to employ all the features that an online version might offer.

First Conversion: To Correspondence. The traditional correspondence version used essentially the same readings as the face-to-face version, but relied on discussion questions and short assignments as substitutes for the discussions and question-and-answer sessions of the face-to-face format. The primary assignment in the course was a multipart project that required students to develop a highly detailed written plan for a short-term program of their own choosing. This project—and the overall course—was organized into six planning elements that corresponded to a generic planning model (Sork, 1997, 2000). Students submitted parts of this project throughout the term and received feedback on earlier parts before submitting later parts, so it fit well with the unit structure of conventional correspondence courses and the principle of giving students fast, periodic feedback throughout the term. The reading material and reinforcing exercises were keyed to each unit, so the readings were directly relevant to the part of the assignment the student was then developing. As new literature became available or as we learned from students that they needed more help with some aspect of planning—and we often learned this from student questions during the course or feedback at the end of the course-we did our best to provide enough readings, examples, and resources for further study so students could produce the quality of work we expected.

The biggest challenges we faced as we developed the conventional correspondence version of the course were (1) how to provide students with the print resources they would need to be successful in the course while keeping to a minimum the telephone calls, e-mails, and other requests for support received by tutors and (2) how to schedule the work in a way that took into account the uncertainties of when assignments would be received, how long it would take tutors to assess them, and how quickly the students would receive feedback. Of course, this all occurred when regular mail was the primary means of communication, supplemented with telephone calls during tutor office hours and, later, e-mails.

New Directions for Adult and Continuing Education • DOI: 10.1002/ace

In 2002, the support unit that administers all diploma programs in the UBC Faculty of Education recommended that we simultaneously update all the adult education courses and convert them to an online format using WebCT. This was good timing for us for three reasons. First, we knew that prospective students were now expecting easier access from a distance to a wider range of courses, and this was the case with those interested in our diploma programs. Second, we had just enrolled the first students in our new online ALGC program and needed some online elective courses for these students. Third, the correspondence versions of these courses were looking dated, not so much because their content was dated but because they did not take advantage of the Web for delivery. This made them harder to access for students and more difficult to update, and it unnecessarily extended the turnaround time on assignments that is so important to minimize in order for effective learning to occur. Another happy coincidence was that a new edition of the textbook used in the course (Caffarella, 2002) was just out, so our revision would reflect the most recent literature.

Second Conversion: To Online. Two graduates of our adult education master's program—both with considerable experience teaching Web-based courses—had been tutoring the correspondence version for several years, so we enlisted their help. First, we identified what needed to be changed in the content of the course to reflect the new edition of the text, but also to supplement the text. Second, we discussed at length the strengths and limitations of the primary assignment and whether it should be retained as we moved the course onto the Web. One key feature of the assignment that concerned us was that it did not involve any kind of collaboration. The independent nature of this project was a carryover from both the face-to-face and correspondence versions. We knew from the literature the advantages of collaborative learning (Brookfield, 1986; Bruffee, 1987) and also knew that moving online would give us the opportunity to have virtual discussions of the kind we had in the face-to-face course, which were absent in the correspondence version. Of course, one of the great advantages of online delivery is the potential for collaborative learning, but we faced a decision about whether to incorporate collaborative assignments into the course structure. Several considerations led to our final decision, which was to retain the independent nature of the primary assignment while incorporating virtual discussions on topics that seemed to raise the most questions for students. We were concerned about the workload of the tutors—a key practical consideration in going online. We wanted the online time of the tutors to be focused on topics that were not adequately explained in the readings. These were relatively easy to identify from questions that had been posed by students in the correspondence version and problems that had appeared with some regularity in assignments. Once this was done, we were able to structure online discussions so that students could engage in a virtual, guided conversation about some of the more challenging aspects of planning and then apply what they learned to their individual projects. This approach is in contrast to case 1, where from the outset it was the intention to encourage as much interaction as possible throughout the course and where at least one collaborative assignment was required.

One great advantage to going online and having students submit their assignments electronically is that those who wish can share their work with others, both before they submit a unit—to receive formative feedback and advice from their peers—and after, as a way to share illustrations of the variety of ways that plans can be developed and presented.

It remains to be seen whether we have incorporated enough interaction and collaborative work into the online version of the course to satisfy most students. We have found in our experience with online learning that students have widely varying levels of interest in the more collaborative aspects of online learning (just as they do with collaborative activities in face-to-face courses), so structuring a level of interaction that will be satisfying for most students will require some experimentation.

When taking what is considered a successful face-to-face course online, it is tempting to retain as many of the original course's features as possible, even though this might not produce the best online experience for students. WebCT, Blackboard, and other online course management systems offer many choices of how to engage students in the learning process. We followed a conservative approach to taking this course online, using only a few of the features offered by WebCT. As we receive feedback from students and review how well the online version seems to be working, we will likely incorporate other features to enhance the learning experience. The advantage of a conservative approach is that it provides an opportunity to learn how various features work, the degree to which they enhance the learning experience, and their implications for workload.

Summary. This case is an example of the conversion of a face-to-face planning course to a traditional correspondence course and subsequently to online format. In discussing this case, we illustrate the shifts that must occur in how student-instructor and student-student relationships are understood when traditional courses are converted for Web-based delivery.

Taken together, the two cases discussed in this chapter indicate that flexibility is one of the keys to success when converting a face-to-face course for online delivery. An ability to be flexible in how tasks are developed and delivered is important, as is asking students for regular feedback to find out what is working and what is not working. And, of course, instructors need the courage to be prepared to change if something is not working as intended.

Implications for Adult and Continuing Education

Educational institutions and private companies are moving to online delivery of courses and programs at an increasing pace. But as the number of online courses increases, the challenges in their development and delivery become more apparent and have implications for adult and continuing education. The increasing recognition and importance of lifelong learning suggests that in the future, adults will seek Web-based programs that deliver access to educational opportunities at locations and times convenient to them.

Converting traditional classroom courses for online delivery is not a simple or linear process. The process requires analysis of the curriculum to determine the appropriate conversion process, development of online course materials, and implementation of the plan. Beyond the conversion of textual materials, there is a need to be cognizant of the shifts that will occur in how student-instructor and student-student relationships are understood when traditional courses are converted for Web-based delivery.

The increasing number of adults participating in adult and continuing education requires the development of more and better programs, delivered using new instructional techniques, to reach people using distance education delivery methods. There is a need to know more about adult instructional techniques and ways to enhance learners' engagement in online and distance learning settings. Educators need to help adult learners recognize and improve their self-directed learning capabilities, evaluate their own competencies, and develop plans to satisfy their individual learning needs.

References

Abrandt Dahlgren, M., Larsson, S., and Walters, S. "Making the Invisible Visible: On Participation and Communication in a Global, Web-Based Master's Program." *Higher Education*, 2006, 52(1), 69–93.

Brookfield, S. D. *Understanding and Facilitating Adult Learning.* San Francisco: Jossey-Bass, 1986.

Bruffee, K. A. "The Art of Collaborative Learning." *Change*, 1987, 19(2), 42–47.

Caffarella, R. S. *Planning Programs for Adult Learners: A Practical Guide for Educators, Trainers and Staff Developers.* (2nd ed.) San Francisco: Jossey-Bass, 2002.

Larsson, S., and others. "Confronting Globalization: Learning from Intercontinental Collaboration." *Innovations in Education and Teaching International*, 2005, 42(1), 61–71.

Sork, T. J. "Workshop Planning." In J. A. Fleming (ed.), New Perspectives on Designing and Implementing Effective Workshops. New Directions for Adult and Continuing Education, no. 76. San Francisco: Jossey-Bass, 1997.

Sork, T. J. "Planning Educational Programs." In A. L. Wilson and E. R. Hayes (eds.), *Handbook of Adult and Continuing Education.* (New ed.) San Francisco: Jossey-Bass, 2000.

GARNET GROSJEAN *is a lecturer in adult education and a senior research fellow at the Centre for Policy Studies in Higher Education and Training, University of British Columbia.*

THOMAS J. SORK *is professor of adult education at the University of British Columbia.*

3

*This chapter describes online consensus group work, a
form of collaborative learning. It discusses collaborative
learning, small group work, and consensus learning, with
recommendations for their use in online contexts.*

Using Consensus Groups in Online Learning

Regina O. Smith, John M. Dirkx

In a recent conversation, India, a middle-aged white woman in a graduate
course on adult learning, reflected on her experiences in an online collaborative learning group:

> We all have such different opinions that it's exciting. We all really have the same
> ideas but verbally we come from very different places and we all agree. It's when
> we get to writing; everybody writes well but we don't really write as a group. . .
> . It's like pulling teeth . . . the group is so diverse that it can be quite a challenge
> to get things done and I can't think. Everybody comes to the group with their
> different individual learning styles. Now you've got the kid, if you like, who is
> just there for the grade. You've got the stressed out single mother who barely
> makes it to class because they can't get childcare, and it gets canceled at the last
> minute, so they are arriving not in a learning mode. You've got the over achiev-
> ers like me. And you've just got the kind of average [student]. . . . Sometimes I
> think it's maybe an inter-generational thing. . . . So then we are given these tasks
> to do. . . . So you have this pile of spaghetti and then you throw in the subject
> matter, which is in this instance, adult learning. And you know the theory is
> everywhere. So there are two mixes of spaghetti. Then on top of that, some peo-
> ple have got a background in psychology and some people haven't. . . . My final
> part is you throw in the fact that we're not having a class in adult learning the-
> ory just to get us going. We actually learn it as we go along. . . . But, many times,
> I put my ideas out there, and no one responds. So this is my bowl of spaghetti
> and that all gets stirred up together. To me I look in it and I go I don't know
> where to start. And that's when I can't think [Smith, 2003, p. 96].

NEW DIRECTIONS FOR ADULT AND CONTINUING EDUCATION, no. 113, Spring 2007 © 2007 Wiley Periodicals, Inc.
Published online in Wiley InterScience (www.interscience.wiley.com) • DOI: 10.1002/ace244

As the number of online learning programs in higher and adult education escalates, scholars and practitioners have turned their attention to the quality of the learning environment that characterizes this medium. Early online courses, which essentially represented electronic versions of old correspondence courses (Boshier, Mohapi, and Boulton, 1997), suffered from soaring attrition rates that many attributed to feelings of isolation and lack of student motivation engendered by the environment (Bullen, 1998). To counteract this trend, scholars and practitioners advocated the use of collaborative learning environments (Bullen, 1998; Harasim, 1987). Recently researchers have begun to focus on student interactions and perceptions of their experiences within these online collaborative environments (Palloff and Pratt, 2005). For example, the February 2002 issue of *Distance Education Journal* is devoted to the use of online problem-based learning, a form of collaborative learning, and the February 2005 issue of *Studies in Higher Education* is devoted to small online consensus-type groups.

In this chapter, we describe the use of online consensus group work (CGW), a form of collaborative learning. There are many forms of collaborative group work, such as peer tutoring, writing peer groups, project-based learning, problem-based learning, and case-based learning, but the consensus group represents a central attribute of most of these variations (Bruffee, 1999). Collaborative learning, as we are using it here, needs to be differentiated from cooperative learning. Cooperative learning (Cohen, 1986; Johnson and Johnson, 1978) involves individual effort (Bruffee, 1999) but brings students together in small groups to work on specific well-defined and well-structured problems and questions. The overall focus is on mastery of a body of knowledge. For the most part, students work with well-defined rules and remain under the direction and control of the teacher (Bruffee, 1999). Although collaborative learning shares many of the characteristics of cooperative learning, it requires small groups to confront complex, real-life situations in ill-structured problems (Bruffee, 1999). The goal of the group work is to shift the locus of control in the learning setting from the teacher to student peer groups (Abercrombie, 1960; Bruffee, 1999). Learners are entrusted with the ability to govern themselves (Bruffee, 1999; Gerlach, 1994; Flannery, 1994) in an effort to help them acknowledge dissent and disagreement and cope with difference and ambiguity.

Scholars (see, for example, Harasim, 1987; McKnight, 2000) cite several advantages of the online environment that make it ideal for collaborative learning. The ongoing nature of asynchronous group meetings negates the need to coordinate schedules to meet with group members (McConnell, 2000). Contextualized content and active learning strategies within collaborative learning approaches result in increased learner motivation, persistence, and learning outcomes. Proponents maintain that as students work

New Directions for Adult and Continuing Education • DOI: 10.1002/ace

in groups, they foster a community of learners in which all voices are shared and respected, thus allowing students to feel connected to one another, the teacher, and the content.

While CGW makes heavy use of subject matter, the focus is on using the content to help individual learners address the assigned problem rather than master it. As students work in small, heterogeneous groups, they learn the subject matter content, appropriate problem-solving and critical thinking skills, and skills necessary to work together collaboratively (Abercrombie, 1960; Bruffee, 1999; Flannery, 1994). Students are considered co-constructors of knowledge (Bruffee, 1999) rather than just consumers of it.

The consensus process provides an opportunity for all group members to express their opinions and feel that they have been heard (Ball Foundation, 2002). Consensus is critical to the CGW process (Abercrombie, 1960; Bruffee, 1999) because it is only through consensus that group members are required to listen, hear, understand, and finally accept the viewpoint of group peers. When students are forced, through dialogue and deliberation, to come to consensus, they must work harder to consider all viewpoints in order to reach agreement (Gerlach, 1994; Flannery, 1994). In CGW, students call into question, through iterative cycles of discussion and reflection, the assumptions, values, beliefs, symbols, and rules of conduct that characterize their existing ways of meaning making. Through this process, students learn to integrate individual perspectives with relevant theory and research to promote changes in beliefs that are more inclusive than previous beliefs. The process promotes reflection-in-action (Schön, 1990), which is characteristic of how adults function in their professional lives. Theoretically CGW embodies many of the principles and tenets that have historically characterized the nature of adult learning, including participatory democratic social spaces that empower students, provide a space for reflection, and promote changes in worldview.

Using Consensus Groups to Foster Online Learning

CGW may be used within a variety of instructional contexts to address differing learning objectives. Common to these various contexts are several characteristics: the larger class is divided into smaller groups, each group is assigned a task, the groups negotiate a consensus around the task, and each group explicitly evaluates the quality of its work (Bruffee, 1999). In some instances, the individual groups report out to the larger group and pursue consensus within the larger group around the assigned task.

We have used CGW within an online problem-based learning (PBL) context. The use of PBL actually reflects several models (Saven-Baden, 2000), each with its own assumptions about learning objectives and ways to address these objectives. Our use of PBL reflects the conventional and well-established use of small groups of students charged with analyzing an

New Directions for Adult and Continuing Education • DOI: 10.1002/ace

ill-structured practice scenario, coming to consensus about the nature of the problem central to the scenario, and collectively developing some recommended actions to address the perceived causes of the problem (Bridges and Hallinger, 1995). To address their assigned task, the groups typically employ consensus decision making to define the problem and arrive at a product aimed at addressing the problem.

Forming Groups. In online CGW, attention to the formation and composition of the groups represents a critical aspect of the process. In the PBL use of CGW, the aim is to maximize the heterogeneity and diversity of the small groups. Diversity is desired because of the need for the group to make use of as many ideas and perspectives as possible in framing and addressing the problem. Thus, attention is paid to the characteristics of the group members: race, gender, age, educational backgrounds, and practice experience related to the focus of the course, for example. Attending to these characteristics assumes that these differences at times result in different ways of perceiving and understanding the case scenarios and issues.

In online CGW, the size of the small group is also a critical consideration. In descriptions of collaborative methods, recommendations for group size vary considerably. When CGW is being used for face-to-face PBL, experienced practitioners recommend groups of no larger than five or six members (Bridges and Hallinger, 1995). To help ameliorate the logistics of online group work in online PBL contexts, we recommend group sizes no larger than three to four. Members of these groups have to agree on acceptable and useful ways of interacting and "meeting" together (whether in chatrooms, telephone conversations, e-mail, or asynchronous discussion boards). Often members of these groups may be separated by time zone differences of five to seven hours or even more. As working adults, their schedules are often radically different, and it is difficult to find common periods in which they might virtually come together. Finally, the great bulk of interactions that occur among team members takes place through writing and posting messages. Having too many members can overwhelm team members with the numbers of posts and e-mails they need to read and respond to.

Another consideration in forming online CGW groups is the duration of the group. Often practitioners form and dissolve groups within a single class period or a given class project or activity. In CGW, however, groups are kept together for longer time periods, often stretching across one or more academic semesters. CGW is used in part to provide participants with the opportunity to learn from and through the group process, as well as the content and the assigned problem or task. Decision making through consensus is a high standard to meet, and many who participate in the process experience considerable frustration around group process, which can be emotional and even somewhat volatile. Yet it is this very process that becomes such a powerful educative experience in CGW. Through this process, participants begin to develop deeper insights into what it takes to work collab

New Directions for Adult and Continuing Education • DOI: 10.1002/ace

oratively with others, the complexities of teamwork and interpersonal inter-action, and insights about themselves as team members. They learn about the importance of attending to group process issues and the ways in which these processes change and develop over time. Because this process is online, participants are able to reflect more on these process issues. Their interactions are not only often separated by time and distance, but they are also recorded, providing an ongoing archive of these interactions that they can use to study and analyze their individual and group behaviors. Online CGW provides learners with an immersion experience in the process and the lessons it holds for those interested in developing more collaborative, democratic processes.

In CGW, the instructor form the individual groups. In this process, we first gather as much information as we can from individual participants. We take into consideration prior work experiences that are related to our sub-ject, educational backgrounds, current interests or major areas of study, approximate age, gender, and race or cultural backgrounds. In deciding on group membership, we try to maximize as much as possible the differences across these various categories. For example, we try to avoid placing in the same group two people with a student affairs background, or two people who work in a community adult education setting, two older and experi-enced practitioners, or two persons from an international context. Because men are often grossly underrepresented in our classes, we try to include no more than one man per group. We also take into consideration location of residence. Here we try to minimize time differences in order to reduce the logistical problems associated with working together online.

We obtain this information through several means. Before the course begins or soon after, participants are asked to complete an online needs assessment. In this assessment, which is open only to the instructor, they provide information on their work and educational backgrounds, career goals, reasons for taking the course, and estimates of existing knowledge and skill in the field of adult learning. Within the first few days in which participants log into the course, we ask them to participate in a "getting to know you" activity, which we label, "Who's in the room?" In this activity, we invite participants to share, in an online discussion forum, a little about who they are, their professional responsibilities, their educational goals and interests, and their expectations for the course and one another. In addition, the course management system we use includes a personal profile that stu-dents can create for themselves. The information provided in this profile is open to both instructors and course participants and represents another way for students to share both textual and visual information about themselves.

Facilitating Groups. Consideration should be given to facilitation of online small groups. Facilitators help groups set agendas and timetables, clarify expectations, keep the group on task, encourage balanced participa tion, and summarize and record group work. Depending on the nature of the group, facilitators may also help the groups reflect on and think more critically about the case through the use of probing questions or feedback. Less commonly, facilitators can be involved in assessing individual student performance.

Facilitation of CGW reflects two broad perspectives that revolve primarily around the relationship of the facilitator to others in the group. In face-to-face PBL consensus groups, practitioners often rely on individuals external to the group to help facilitate their work. Usually an external facilitator is assigned several consensus groups with which to work, and the individual floats or rotates from group to group. The facilitator may be a subject matter expert, but this is not a requirement. Often the external facilitator is employed to help with group process issues. As Bruffee (1999) describes, face-to-face consensus groups may also use internal facilitators, usually one of the members of the team who has been selected or volunteered by others in the group to serve in this capacity. Although the actual responsibilities of the internal facilitator need not vary significantly from an external facilitator, internal facilitators are more likely to assume tasks that help keep the group organized, moving, and on task.

In online CGW, it is common for groups to make use of internal facilitators. Although it is possible, we know of no concrete examples in which practitioners are using external facilitators with online consensus groups. In part, this is probably due to the costs and difficulties associated with training and orienting individuals to serve in this role in online contexts, but in large classes with fifty or more students, consensus groups may require the use of trained external facilitators to ensure that the students' experiences are truly educative.

Our experience with online consensus groups has been with smaller classes in which the total number of groups rarely exceeds eight to ten. For this reason, we have chosen to employ facilitators who are members of the group. We encourage the teams to rotate this responsibility with each problem so that everyone in the team experiences the role before they complete the course. Within the first two weeks of the course, we provide both the teams and the individual facilitators with detailed orientations about the nature of the consensus group process and the role of the facilitator in that process, and allow both team members and facilitators practice with this process before engaging the actual cases that comprise the curriculum. Through asynchronous or synchronous forums, internal facilitators help the groups with instrumental tasks, such as developing a time line of action, setting up synchronous chat meetings if they are desired or warranted, suggesting work assignments, checking to see if all tasks have been completed, and ensuring that all team members are participating within the process. Group facilitators are also responsible for leading the group through a debriefing of their process, assessing its strengths and areas for improvement, and they conduct a review of the product that ensued from their collaboration.

New Directions for Adult and Continuing Education • DOI: 10.1002/ace

As we have used CGW in our classes, the role of the instructor is an important dimension of the facilitation process. Unlike Bruffee (1999), who discourages the teacher from hovering around the work of the consensus groups, we consider the instructor's presence online to be critical to the group's work. Our experience suggests that without the strong social presence of the instructor in the online environment, the groups may lose a sense of direction, scope, and even purpose. For this reason, the instructor also serves as a kind of external facilitator to all the groups. While students may not always experience the group process as uniformly positive and comfortable, we hope that most derive from the experience important learning outcomes that result from critical reflection on the problem, the content, the context of their learning experience, and themselves. In addition to being responsible for the overall design and development of online learning activities, we conceptualize the role of the instructor in online CGW as facilitating the development of these learning outcomes.

Important elements of the instructor's role as an external facilitator of CGW include helping the groups to frame the problem, make effective use of additional resources such as appropriate research and theory, further develop and elaborate the nature of the problem, and work through the problem-solving process. For example, in considering a case, a group member might post to the team discussion forum a particular statement of the problem. The instructor reviews this post and finds that the statement seems to blur the lines between the problem, its underlying causes, and what should be done about these issues. The post may not even identify a specific problem. So in a response, the facilitator teases out these various elements in the group's post and then asks the team for further clarification and restatement of the problem. At times, a member might post to the team forum a set of issues that he or she believes is contributing to the problem or a set of recommendations to address the problem, but the analysis is not grounded in appropriate research and theory or relies too heavily on a single source. The instructor will ask for additional evidence from the literature to support the claims being made here. This process of facilitation always involves first stressing the strengths of the analysis or observations offered so far. Then, building on this recognition of capacity, the instructor may challenge the team or individuals with additional questions that serve to deepen their analysis or use of evidence.

In addition, the instructor helps individuals and groups attend to and learn from the process. Through attention to the process, learners develop higher-order thinking skills, as well as important interpersonal and teamwork skills. The instructor contributes to this role by attending to posts, e-mail, and chatroom discussions; providing constructive feedback; and coaxing further reflection and analysis through probing questions. For example, two members of a three-person group might be forging ahead with a perceptive analysis of the problem. In reviewing the posts, the instructor notices that one of the members has not participated much in this analysis. He or she then posts back to the team support for the analysis but also a query as to whether they have obtained feedback from all their members.

Finally, the instructor helps the group by facilitating group process. Strong disagreements and even conflict are not uncommon in CGW, so instructors need to attend to the manifestation of such processes and issues within the online environment and encourage the group to constructively address these issues rather than ignore or minimize them. Unfortunately, we know relatively little about this important dimension of online learning. Attending to group process in online environments is an emerging area within higher and adult education, and one in need of considerable research and theory (McConnell, 2005).

For example, a member e-mails the instructor that she is concerned with the overall work of the group and is worried that they will not produce quality work. The instructor e-mails back, asking for clarification and specifics. When the student responds with a more detailed description of the concern, the instructor e-mails back, asking the student if she has shared these concerns with her team. If not, and that is usually the case, the instructor recommends that she first express her concerns constructively to her team and try to engage them in a discussion around these issues. We also suggest that if this does not work, we would be willing to set up a conference call with the team members to talk through in real time some of the issues. We have, however, never had to resort to this strategy. In the great majority of instances, this type of intervention addresses the individual's concerns, and the group is able to move forward. As a result of this process, both the individual and the group take responsibility for their own processes and feel empowered to address similar issues in the future.

Effectiveness. Our research on student perceptions of their experiences revealed that students felt they learned more about the content than they could have learned on their own (Smith, 2003). In addition, the students noted several instances when they were able to look at the problem through numerous perspectives, which promoted their ability to think more critically about the course content. The students began to learn how to work more effectively with their group members by recognizing and owning their role in the group conflict and correcting their behavior. For example, one student noted that she was dominating the conversation, so she pulled back and allowed her group members space to participate. A number of students indicated that the ill-structured problems were real; they had experienced the same issues in their work. One group actually used the group product to present to her administrators.

Limitations. Differences among students can generate high levels of frustration, as seen in the quotation at the beginning of the chapter. In our work (for example, see Dirkx and Smith, 2004; Smith, 2003, 2005), we have noted that frustration left students feeling overwhelmed and unsure how to proceed. Often they seek to avoid engaging their differences and use several strategies that seek to avoid the conflict associated with differences. These strategies include imposing rules on what is considered appropriate conclusions about the problem and the readings and forming subgroups of like-minded individuals in the group, which marginalizes students who do not agree with their opinions. In many cases, the students who are marginalized are often those from traditionally marginalized populations based on age, gender, race, and background. Students note that the differences seem insurmountable at times.

Implications for Adult Education

The emotional difficulties that students experience working across difference to reach consensus cause many scholars to caution against using consensus and recommend alternatives to consensus (see, for example, Hodgson and Reynolds, 2005). Other scholars (Meyers and Brashers, 2002) cite the need to help students learn to argue in productive ways that negate the need to use the strategies that prevent them from collaborating. Although we recognize the tremendous challenge that CGW presents for all instructors and students, we have also witnessed the potential for growth and development in students. The critical consensus process enables group members to truly listen to values, beliefs, and behaviors that are different from their own. This process fosters the ability to learn from and with difference rather than marginalizing difference.

CGW also draws attention to the social, political, and psychodynamic complexities of developing online community, collaboration, and group work. The ongoing discussion among peers provides a social space for learning. From a political perspective, adult educators face a paradox. On the one hand, the consensus process offers tremendous potential. On the other hand, traditionally marginalized students continue to face even more marginalization in the CGW. Yet if the instructor is attentive to the group process and helps the students work through the difficulty, the marginalization is decreased, and all students learn their role in creating inequities within the learning environment. Finally, CGW provides group members opportunities to study deep process and structures of small group work that is often unconscious and thus invisible to the group. The conflict that results from the different perspectives points to unconscious and unresolved (psychodynamic) issues that members bring to the group that prevent it from moving forward to productive work. In our work, some of these differences reflected issues of gender, race, age, and ability that members used to prejudge group members. Although not all of the issues were involved, when these issues surface in the group, the members have an opportunity to address them.

Our experience demonstrates that if instructors can allow the group to deal with ambiguity without stepping in to solve the problem, students can grow from their political conflict. There is a very fine line between too few and too many interventions, so it is critical to conduct additional research to help adult educators more fully understand their role in this environment.

References

Abercrombie, M. L. *Anatomy of Judgment*. New York: Basic Books, 1960.

Ball Foundation. "Education Initiatives." 2002. Retrieved Nov. 12, 2004, from http://www.ballfoundation.org/ei/tools/consensus.html.

Boshier, R., Mohapi, M., and Boulton, G. "Best and Worst Dressed Web Courses: Strutting into the Twenty-First Century in Comfort and Style." *Distance Education*, 1997, *18*(2), 327–349.

Bridges, E. M., and Hallinger, P. *Implementing Problem-Based Learning in Leadership Development*. Eugene, Ore.: ERIC Clearinghouse on Educational Management, 1995.

Bruffee, K. A. *Collaborative Learning: Higher Education, Interdependence, and the Authority of Knowledge*. (2nd ed.) Baltimore, Md.: Johns Hopkins University Press, 1999.

Bullen, M. "Participation and Critical Thinking in Online University Distance Education." *Journal of Distance Education*, 1998, *13*(2). Retrieved July 14, 2006, from http://cade.athabascau.ca/vol13.2/bullen.html.

Cohen, E. *Designing Groupwork: Strategies for the Heterogeneous Classroom*. New York: Teachers College Press, 1986.

Dirkx, J. M., and Smith, R. O. "Thinking Out of a Bowl of Spaghetti: Learning to Learn in Online Collaborative Groups." In T. Roberts (ed.), *Online Collaborative Learning: Theory and Practice*. Hershey, Pa.: Idea Group, 2004.

Flannery, J. L. "Teacher as Co-Conspirator: Knowledge and Authority in Collaborative Learning." In K. Bosworth and S. J. Hamilton (eds.), *Collaborative Learning: Underlying Process and Effective Techniques*. New Directions for Teaching and Learning, no. 59. San Francisco: Jossey-Bass, 1994.

Gerlach, J. M. "Is This Collaboration?" In K. Bosworth and S. J. Hamilton (eds.), *Collaborative Learning: Underlying Processes and Effective Techniques*. New Directions for Teaching and Learning, no. 59. San Francisco: Jossey-Bass, 1994.

Harasim, L. "Teaching and Learning On-Line: Issues in Computer-Mediated Graduate Courses." *Canadian Journal of Educational Communication*, 1987, *16*(2), 117–135.

Hodgson, V., and Reynolds, M. "Consensus, Difference and Multiple Communities in Networked Learning." *Studies in Higher Education*, 2005, *30*(1), 11–24.

Johnson, R. W., and Johnson, R. T. "Cooperative, Competitive, and Individualistic Learning." *Journal of Research and Development in Education*, 1978, *12*(1), 65–95.

McConnell, D. *Implementing Computer Supported Cooperative Learning*. (2nd ed.) London: Kogan Page, 2000.

McConnell, D. "Examining the Dynamics of Networked e-Learning Groups and Communities." *Studies in Higher Education*, 2005, *30*(1) 24–42.

McKnight, C. "Teaching Critical Thinking Through Online Discussions." *Educause Quarterly*, 2000, *4*, 38–41.

Meyers, R. A., and Brashers, D. E. "Rethinking Traditional Approaches to Argument in Groups." In L. R. Frey (ed.), *New Directions in Group Communication*. Thousand Oaks, Calif.: Sage, 2002.

Palloff, R. M., and Pratt, K. *Collaborating Online: Learning Together in Community*. San Francisco: Jossey-Bass, 2005.

Saven-Baden, M. *Problem-Based Learning in Higher Education: Untold Stories*. Bristol, Pa.: Society for Research into Higher Education and Open University Press, 2000.

Schön, D. Educating the Reflective Practitioner. San Francisco: Jossey-Bass, 1990.

Smith, R. O. "The Struggle for Voice: Student Experiences in Collaborative Online Groups." Unpublished doctoral dissertation, Michigan State University, 2003.

Smith, R. O. "Working with Difference in Online Collaborative Groups." *Adult Education Quarterly*, 2005, 55(3), 182–199.

REGINA O. SMITH is an assistant professor of adult and continuing education at the University of Wisconsin-Milwaukee.

JOHN M. DIRKX is a professor of higher, adult, and lifelong education at Michigan State University, East Lansing, Michigan.

Concept maps are an instructional strategy that promotes meaningful learning. This chapter examines the use of concept maps in online environments through discussion of CmapTools software.

CmapTools: Integrating Teaching, Learning, and Evaluation in Online Courses

Barbara J. Daley, Alberto J. Cañas, Tracy Stark-Schweitzer

Teaching, learning, and evaluation in online courses offer unique and exciting challenges for instructors. Not only is it necessary to find new teaching strategies in an online environment, but it is also imperative that instructors find ways to facilitate student learning and structure evaluation strategies that support and promote a deeper and more meaningful type of learning. Concept maps (Novak, 1998) are one strategy that can promote teaching, learning, and evaluation in online environments.

Creating Concept Maps

As Novak and Gowin (1984) indicate, "A concept map is a schematic device for representing a set of concept meanings in a framework of propositions" (p. 15). Concept maps are pictures or graphical representations that learners draw to depict their understanding of the meaning of a set of concepts. They use the maps to link new learning to what they already know. In this way, the maps offer learners and instructors an opportunity to share, dis-

---

Note: CmapTools is available for free for nonprofit use from http://cmap.ihmc.us.

NEW DIRECTIONS FOR ADULT AND CONTINUING EDUCATION, no. 113, Spring 2007 © 2007 Wiley Periodicals, Inc.
Published online in Wiley InterScience (www.interscience.wiley.com) • DOI: 10.1002/ace.245

cuss, and revise their understanding of concepts, propositions, and the relationships between new and existing knowledge. Concept maps can be used to foster conceptual learning, critical thinking, analysis, synthesis, and the development of shared meaning.

Constructing a concept map has these steps:

1. Define a focus question, that is, a question that clearly specifies the problem or issue that the concept map should resolve (Novak and Cañas, 2006a).
2. Identify and list the key fifteen to twenty-five concepts that apply to the knowledge domain of the map.
3. Rank-order these concepts from the most general, inclusive concept for the problem or situation to the most specific, least general concept. This ranking will most likely be approximate.
4. Start building a preliminary concept map by taking concepts out of this list (which we refer to as the parking lot) to determine where they fit in.
5. As the concept map is built, tie the concepts together with linking words in some fashion that makes sense or has meaning.
6. After the preliminary map is constructed, look for cross-linkages among the different segments or domains of knowledge on the map, illustrating how these domains are related to one another.
7. Share, discuss, and revise the map, understanding that a concept map is never really finished.

Figure 4.1 depicts a simple concept map created by a student. The focus question for this student's map was intended to demonstrate a beginning understanding of how the literature on adult and women's cognitive development is related.

Concept maps can be drawn by hand or developed using software packages (such as CmapTools) designed for this purpose. Concept maps as a learning strategy are based on a strong body of theoretical and research knowledge.

Concept Mapping: Theoretical and Research Base

Concept maps are based on Ausubel, Novak, and Hanesian's assimilation theory of learning (1986). Within this theoretical framework, the learner shifts away from learning in a rote fashion and moves to learning in a more meaningful, connected fashion. Rather than memorizing information, the learner searches out the relationships among concepts and organizes a structure to the new knowledge that is unique to him or her. The learner accomplishes this by linking new information learned to existing knowledge and experiences.

New Directions for Adult and Continuing Education • DOI: 10.1002/ace

According to assimilation theory, we use concepts to learn in three ways. First, we learn by subsuming lower-order concepts under higher-order concepts. In this process, the learner identifies broad general concepts and then finds more specific concepts related to the general concepts. The learner may learn the broad concept first and then find the relationship of the more specific concepts, or the learner may initially develop an understanding of the more specific concepts, eventually relating those to the broader concept. Either way, the learner is using both inductive and deductive thinking processes in structuring conceptual relationships.

Figure 4.1. Simple Student Concept Map Developed with Cmap Tools

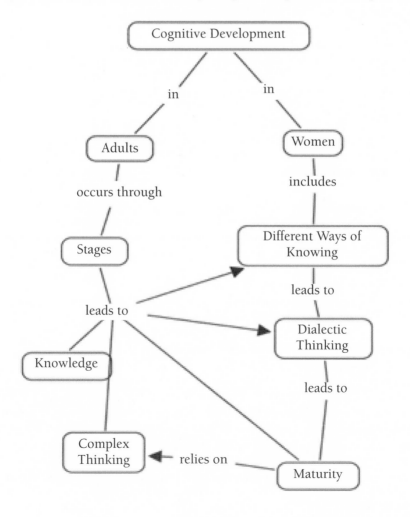

Table 4.1. Recent Literature on Concept Mapping

Study	Purpose of the Study	Findings
Boxtel, Linden, Roelofs, and Erkens (2002)	Examined collaborative concept-mapping tasks as a learning tool	Group concept mapping showed significant learning gains.
Cañas and others (2003)	A comprehensive literature review on the use of concept mapping and technologies	Concept maps facilitate learning across disciplines and facilitate capture of conceptual knowledge. Technologies such as CmapTools enhance concept mapping by providing a network to facilitate collaboration.
Daley (2002)	Investigated the ways concept maps influenced the thinking of adult students	Findings indicate that students' map scores increased significantly over the course of a semester and remained at the same level a year later.
Daley and others (1999)	Examined concepts maps as a strategy to teach and evaluate critical thinking	A significant increase in student concept map scores was found. Scores demonstrated changes in conceptual and critical thinking.
Edmondson and Smith (1998)	Examined concept mapping as a strategy to facilitate students' understanding of various topics	Students reported that their understanding was greatly facilitated through the use of concept maps. Faculty saw concept mapping as a strategy for better long-term retention.
Kinchin and Hay (2000)	Explored qualitative methods as an analysis strategy for concept mapping	Classification patterns and themes gained through qualitative methods posed teaching strategies for more effective learning.
Laight (2004)	Examined student attitudes about concept mapping as an innovative learning resource	A significant number of students reported that preprepared concept maps were a useful learning resource.
West and others (2000)	Examined whether concept-mapping assessment of residents demonstrates expected changes in their conceptual frameworks	Expected differences and changes in the residents were demonstrated.
West and others (2002)	Assessed the validity of two concept-mapping scoring methods: a structural and a relational method	The structural scoring method showed a significant increase in concept map scores. There was no significant difference in relational scores.

Second, we learn by progressively differentiating concepts into more and more complex understandings. This process involves the analysis of concepts and breaking down those concepts into component parts. For example, a beginning medical student might differentiate the concept of pneumonia into symptoms that include chills, cough, fever, chest pain, and shortness of breath. Third, we learn through a process of integrative reconciliation. This final process involves synthesizing and understanding concepts by finding linkages and connections across bodies of knowledge. For example, the beginning medical student may link the symptoms of pneumonia to other concepts, such as medical history, medications, and various therapies, to come up with a comprehensive plan of care for the client.

In addition to the theoretical underpinnings of concept maps, there is a large research base on which the use of concept maps is based. This research was initiated by Joseph Novak and Bob Gowin (1984) in their role as faculty members at Cornell University (Novak and Cañas, 2006b). In his early work, Novak (1990) conducted a twelve-year study of concept development and used concept maps as a way to show the changes in students' thinking. In this study, clinical interviews were completed with students in grade 2 and through their school years up to grade 12. The study demonstrated growth in both the number and relationships of concept meanings over this span of time. Since the time of this study, a vast research base on concept mapping has been developed in various disciplines, including education, the natural sciences, nursing, medicine, veterinary science, social work, business, and adult education. The majority of these studies indicate that concept maps have value in the facilitation of learning, the development of knowledge structures, and understanding relationships among concepts.

Table 4.1 lists a number of recent and cross-disciplinary empirical studies and conceptual articles that inform concept mapping. Although these studies are different methodologically, several common themes emerged from the findings. In addition, the studies vary notably in purpose and method and thus illustrate the broad applicability of concept mapping in educational settings, including adult and online education.

What emerges from an analysis of Table 4.1 is that concept maps facilitate a change in learning and thinking in a wide variety of learners and that this change appears to be maintained over time. In addition, it appears that concept maps can assist in group learning and can provide a measure of evaluation and assessment of learning. Finally, it appears that software programs facilitate the creation and sharing of concept maps.

CmapTools

For adult learners in online courses, constructing a concept map without a digital tool is like writing a long essay without a word processor: most of us do not even remember how we prepared and edited long documents with out the facility to modify them easily on the screen. Building a concept map is an iterative process. For example, deciding on the linking phrase that best depicts the relationship between two concepts often takes some time and many trials. Thus, a software program like CmapTools (Cañas and others, 2004) makes it extremely easy to move the concepts and links around the screen, so users can concentrate on the important aspects: organizing the concepts and linking phrases without having to worry about the mechanics.

CmapTools has been designed to be much more than a concept map editing tool. It is meant to support a concept map-centered learning environment, where the concept map is not seen as an add-on activity but as the glue that can link together all of the student's work (Cañas and Novak, 2005). From an initial map constructed by a student to determine how much he or she knows at the beginning of a study unit (which often shows an incomplete understanding or misconceptions, or both), we propose that the map be refined as the student progresses, demonstrating how the student's understanding deepens. For example, the student may use the concept map as an initial step in doing research on the topic being studied: CmapTools provides a search mechanism that allows the student to right-click on a concept and search for information on the Web that is related to that concept and that map specifically (Carvalho, Hewett, and Cañas, 2001). Studying the retrieved information will lead to a better map or to the construction of other concept maps linked to the original one. This new map will provide for a more precise search, leading to an iterative research and refinement process. Maps constructed from readings could complement or be linked to the original map. As the learning progresses, the collection of

Figure 4.2. Concept Map with Some Linked Resources Displayed

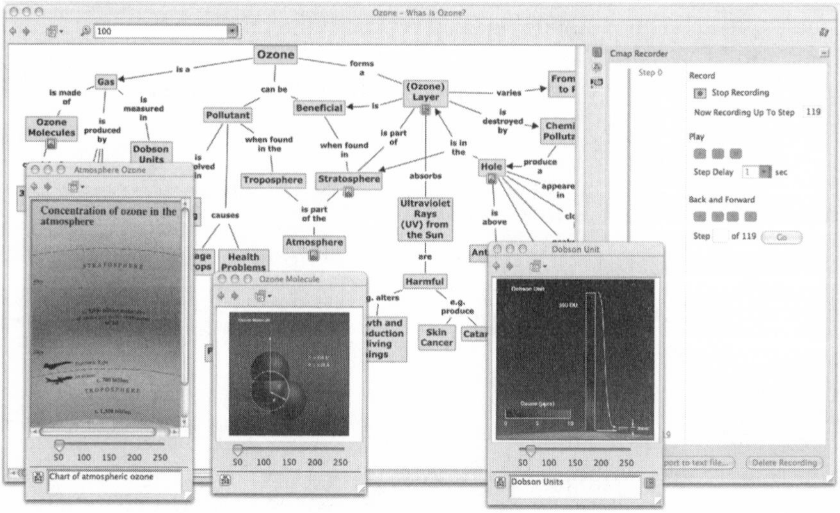

concept maps and linked resources on the topic (referred to as a knowledge model) will reflect the increased understanding on the part of the learner. Figure 4.2 shows a concept map with attached resources, which are linked through icons under the concepts. The Recorder pane on the right in the figure has controls that enable a playback of the steps taken in constructing the map. CmapTools is particularly rich in features to support collaboration and teamwork. On CmapServers (computers on the Internet where users can store their maps and automatically publish them as Web pages), students can modify their maps from anywhere on the Internet, collaborate on the construction of their knowledge models, and even edit the maps synchronously from distant locations. Through annotations and discussion threads, students can comment, critique, and peer-review each other's map. Instructors can also access and comment on a student's maps. A presentation module allows students and instructors to use the concept maps and attached resources to present their results full-screen instead of decomposing their maps into PowerPoint bullets. Collaboration is easily facilitated because the CmapTools program and the CmapTools servers can be linked to any course management system, such as Blackboard or Desire2Learn.

CmapTools also provides features aimed mainly at the instructor. The CmapRecorder allows a step-by-step playback of the map construction process, so the instructor can see the process students used to build the map. A comparison utility allows graphical comparison of the content of two concept maps; the instructor can compare his or her map to the student's to determine, for example, if all the concepts the instructor gave the student are included in the map. This module is not meant to be an assessment tool, but a tool that initially helps the instructor analyze a student's map. Figure 4.3 shows the result of comparing the concept map from Figure 4.2 with a student's concept map. In Figure 4.3, the matching elements are shown in the lighter-shaded areas. The pane on the right provides a summary of the results and allows users to control the depth and type of comparison.

Using Concept Maps in Teaching, Learning, and Evaluation

CmapTools can be incorporated into any course taught online for adult learners. It is a relatively easy program for students to install and learn. The most effective way to use concept maps to develop thinking and learning is to make them an integral part of the course structure rather than an add-on activity. By this, we mean that the development of concept maps needs to be woven into the learning activities throughout the course. The use of concept maps in online courses promotes a more constructivist type of thinking, and it often takes time for students to develop and expand their thinking in this realm. In addition, many students have never had the opportunity to begin to understand their own thinking and learning processes, a skill that cannot be developed through the use of intermittent concept mapping. Students need multiple mapping experiences to develop the deeper level of meaningful learning that the maps promote.

Analyzing Readings and Developing Papers. One way to promote meaningful learning is to have students construct concept maps of the course readings. When using this strategy, we ask students to pick a reading that piqued their interest in a particular topic and to map out the reading as a way to understand it. We also ask students to demonstrate relationships between two or more readings or two or more authors by developing a concept map. The idea is not to map the documents as they are being read, but to construct the map once the student finishes reading them, to show how much he or she understood and learned. Finally, in many courses, we have students submit a concept map of a paper they plan to write. We then provide feedback on the concept map before the student actually writes the paper. This process helps students conceptualize the paper and understand the relationships they are trying to develop in a different way. This is particularly true for doctoral students who are writing literature reviews. Often a concept map of a literature review helps the student to see the interrelationships of multiple themes in the literature.

Figure 4.3. Graphical Comparison of Two Concept Maps

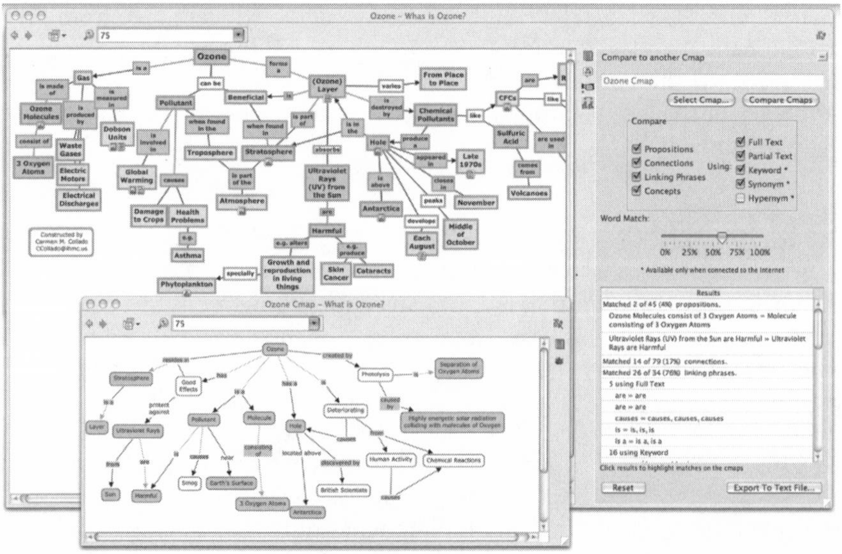

Analyzing Experiences. One of the ways that adult students learn most effectively is in analyzing their own experiences and linking them to the new information they are learning. Concept maps can be used to facilitate the process of learning from experience. For example, in an adult education course, students are asked to create a concept map of their development as an adult. Then they are asked to show specific links on their concept maps between their own unique experiences and the adult development theories we are studying.

Case Studies. The use of case studies can be facilitated with concept maps. In our online course on continuing professional education, we present a case from the field and ask students to work in groups to map out their understanding of that case. Then we proceed through the module for that topic. Students work in online groups to complete and discuss the course readings. At the conclusion of the module, we ask them to develop a second map and show how their understanding of the case has changed based on the new knowledge they have acquired in the module. The process of mapping and remapping the same case assists students in seeing how knowledge can be constructed around cases.

Relating Theory to Practice. Drawing relationships between theory and practice presents difficulty in most disciplines. It is difficult for students to see these complex relationships and sort out the importance and meaning of theory-to-practice connections. Concept maps can help facilitate this process. For example, nursing and medical students in our courses have developed concept maps that depict the care they will provide a client based on their understanding of theories they have learned. Students have developed maps that link the disease process of a client to the treatment plan, medications, and family influences.

Learning in Groups. One of the advantages of developing concept maps in online courses is that adult learners can construct maps within the context of a group of learners. CmapTools contains provisions to develop maps asynchronously or synchronously. In our courses, we have had groups of students develop maps to design a group project or paper, analyze the context of an organization, and conduct a learning needs assessment.

Using Concept Maps to Evaluate and Assess Learning. When students create concept maps, instructors get a glimpse into how their mind is working and how they are constructing knowledge. So not only are the maps a teaching and learning strategy, but they can also be used to provide feedback and assess learning. In our courses, we usually provide feedback on concept maps to students based on Ausubel, Novak, and Hanesian's assimilation theory (1986). We suggest to students how they can subsume lower-order concepts under higher-order concepts and demonstrate both progressive differentiation and integrative reconciliation of concepts.

Challenges in Creating Concept Maps with Adult Learners in Online Courses

In our experience, using concept maps with adult learners in online courses has two challenges. First, it takes adult learners some additional time to feel comfortable with this learning approach. Often adults come to learning situations having been highly successful using certain learning strategies, so asking them to change these strategies can meet with some resistance. Creating concept maps is a new way of thinking, learning, and constructing knowledge that may not initially be comfortable for adults. Thus, they need support and encouragement from the instructor. Second, learners report that they spend more time studying when they create concept maps. What happens here is that before creating a map, learners read, think about the content, talk online with colleagues, and then engage in creating a map. This reflective process in which they engage initially takes them more time, so learners often think that it is the process of creating the map that is taking more of their time. Eventually learners recognize that they are engaging in a deeper learning process.

Conclusion

Using CmapTools in online courses can accomplish all of the teaching and learning strategies we have described. This software provides a way to operationalize the use of concept maps in the online environment, and it assists in making online courses interactive, dynamic, and solidly grounded in theoretical and well-researched teaching and learning theories.

References

Ausubel, D. P., Novak, J. D., and Hanesian, H. *Educational Psychology: A Cognitive View.* (2nd ed.) New York: Werbel and Peck, 1986.

Boxtel, C. V., Linden, J. V., Roelofs, E., and Erkens, G. "Collaborative Concept Mapping: Provoking and Supporting Meaningful Discourse." *Theory into Practice*, 2002, *41*(1), 40–46.

Cañas, A., and others. A Summary of Literature Pertaining to the Use of Concept Mapping Techniques and Technologies for Education and Performance Support. 2003. Pensacola, Fla.: Institute for Human and Machine Cognition, 2003. Retrieved Nov. 1, 2005, from http://www.ihmc.us/users/acanas/Publications/ConceptMapLitReview/IHMC%20Literature%20Review%20on%20Concept%20Mapping.pdf.

Cañas, A. J., and Novak, J. D. "A Concept Map-Centered Learning Environment." Paper presented at the Symposium at the Eleventh Biennial Conference of the European Association for Research in Learning and Instruction, Cyprus, 2005.

Cañas, A. J., and others. "CmapTools: A Knowledge Modeling and Sharing Environment." In A. J. Cañas, J. D. Novak, and F. M. González (eds.), *Concept Maps: Theory, Methodology, Technology: Proceedings of the First International Conference on Concept Mapping*. Pamplona, Spain: Universidad Pública de Navarra, 2004.

Carvalho, M. R., Hewett, R., and Cañas, A. J. "Enhancing Web Searches from Concept Map-Based Knowledge Models." In N. Callaos, F. G. Tinetti, J. M. Champarnaud, and J. K. Lee (eds.), *Proceedings of SCI 2001: Fifth Multiconference on Systems, Cybernetics and Informatics.* Orlando, Fla.: International Institute of Informatics and Systemics, 2001.

Daley, B. "Facilitating Learning with Adult Students Through Concept Mapping." *Journal of Continuing Higher Education,* 2002, *50*(1), 21–31.

Daley, B., and others. "Concept Maps: A Strategy to Teach and Evaluate Critical Thinking." *Journal of Nursing Education,* 1999, *38*(1), 1–6.

Edmondson, K. M., and Smith, D. F. "Concept Mapping to Facilitate Veterinary Students' Understanding of Fluid and Electrolyte Disorders." *Teaching and Learning in Medicine,* 1998, *10*(1), 21–33.

Kinchin, I. M., and Hay, D. B. "How a Qualitative Approach to Concept Map Analysis Can Be Used to Aid Learning by Illustrating Patterns of Conceptual Development." *Educational Research,* 2000, *42*(1), 43–57.

Laight, D. W. "Attitudes to Concept Maps as a Teaching/Learning Activity in Undergraduate Health Professional Education: Influence of Preferred Learning Style." *Medical Teacher,* 2004, *26*(3), 229–233.

Novak, J. *Learning, Creating and Using Knowledge: Concept Maps as Facilitative Tools in Schools and Corporations.* Mahwah, N.J.: Erlbaum, 1998.

Novak, J. D. "Concept Maps and Vee Diagrams: Two Metacognitive Tools to Facilitate Meaningful Learning." *Instructional Science,* 1990, *19,* 29–52.

Novak, J. D., and Cañas, A. J. *The Theory Underlying Concept Maps and How to Construct Them.* Pensacola: Florida Institute for Human and Machine Cognition, 2006a. Retrieved Dec. 26, 2006, from http://cmap.ihmc.us/Publications/ResearchPapers/TheoryUnderlyingConceptMaps.pdf.

Novak, J. D., and Cañas, A. J. "The Origins of Concept Mapping and the Continuing Evolution of the Tool." *Information Visualization Journal,* 2006b. Retrieved Dec. 26, 2006, from http://cmap.ihmc.us/Publications/ResearchPapers/OriginsOfConceptMappingTool.pdf.

Novak, J. D., and Gowin, B. *Learning How to Learn.* Cambridge: Cambridge University Press, 1984.

West, D. C., and others. "Critical Thinking in Graduate Medical Education: A Role for Concept Mapping Assessment?" *Journal of the American Medical Association,* 2000, *284*(9), 1105–1110.

West, D. C., and others. "Concept Mapping Assessment in Medical Education: A Comparison of Two Scoring Systems." *Medical Education,* 2002, *36,* 820–826.

BARBARA J. DALEY is associate professor of adult and continuing education at the University of Wisconsin-Milwaukee.

ALBERTO J. CAÑAS is associate director of the Institute for Human and Machine Cognition in Pensacola, Florida.

TRACY STARK-SCHWEITZER is a doctoral student at the University of Wisconsin-Milwaukee

5

This chapter focuses on the role of online educators as mentors and addresses the potential impact of a mentoring relationship on the development and persistence of adult learners in the online medium.

Mentoring as Holistic Online Instruction

Kimberly R. Burgess

The concept of mentoring is well accepted in most facets of education and business as a vehicle for experienced persons to guide, prepare, and assist novices both personally and professionally. Mentoring is many times seen as a formal process, where mentors and protégés are paired together with norms of interaction, duties, and responsibilities in order for the mentorship to be considered "effective" and "successful" (Hansman, 2000). Others speak of a system of informal mentoring, where mentors and protégés meet and bond through their commonalities (Caffarella, 1993). Fassinger and Hensler-McGinnis (2005) offer a third alternative, facilitated mentoring, which combines the organizational structure of formal mentoring with the naturalness of free selection and the attraction of informal mentoring. No matter what the format is, these definitions of mentoring assume that mentoring consists of a one-on-one relationship that lasts over an extended period of time, where the mentor and protégé journey together through phases of entry to exit (Cohen, 1995; Daloz, 1986; Kram, 1985; Zachary, 2000).

But most interaction between faculty and students is sporadic, sometimes lasting only a semester or two. Students encounter various potential mentors during their educational experience, all with their own personal histories, their own areas of expertise, and their own special gifts that influence the student (see Hiemstra and Brockett, 1998). In the online environ-

NEW DIRECTIONS FOR ADULT AND CONTINUING EDUCATION, no. 113, Spring 2007 © 2007 Wiley Periodicals, Inc.
Published online in Wiley InterScience (www.interscience.wiley.com) • DOI: 10.1002/ace.246

ment, this interaction is complicated by the isolation of both instructor and student in their own space. Despite the brevity of the relationship and the lack of face-to-face contact, mentoring should be expected of all online instructors (Jacobi, 1991). According to English (2000), mentoring can occur "anywhere that an adult is in need of being taught, sponsored, guided, counseled, and befriended by someone who is more experienced" (p. 31). "Even where teacher-student contact lacks the intensity normally associated with mentorship," Daloz (1999) writes, "students can be powerfully affected by their teachers" (p. 22). Marra and Pangborn (2001) say that students "thirst" for such attention from their faculty (p. 35).

It is well documented that effective online instruction requires skills in effectively selecting appropriate content, moderating discussion, and infusing technology (Ascough, 2002). Other skills identified have included group leadership and critically reflective teaching as key facilitator roles in adult learning (Brookfield, 1986; Collison, Elbaum, Haavind, and Tinker, 2000). This chapter seeks to include mentoring as an effective instructional tool in the online education of adults. The inclusion of mentoring practices, particularly when students are new to both the academic program and the online delivery environment or are members of historically disadvantaged groups, acknowledges students' needs both within and beyond the content of the course and situates online instruction as a holistic endeavor.

Functions of Mentors

Traditionally, one of the primary roles of a mentor has been as a socializing agent, helping the less experienced be knowledgeable in, and become a successful part of, the system within which the protégé seeks to exist (Kram, 1985; Levinson and others, 1978). Traditional notions of mentoring have seemed to be focused on a difference of age (Levinson and others, 1978), associating experienced with older and inexperienced with younger, but this is not necessarily so.

The literature cites many benefits of mentoring for the mentors as well as the protégés, as in theory this should be a reciprocal experience (Jacobi, 1991). Most important, protégés show greater commitment to their field, higher satisfaction with their programs, and a willingness to mentor others (Fassinger and Hensler-McGinnis, 2005). Mentors, particularly in nontraditional adult settings, benefit from the pockets of wisdom and life experiences that students possess (English, 2000). Fassinger and Hensler-McGinnis (2005) caution, though, that older students may overlook and disregard the greater knowledge of a younger instructor simply because he or she does not fit the norm. Recently, however, paradigms of mentoring have shifted toward a collaborative, learning partnership, where the mentor is both benefactor and recipient of learning in the relationship (Hansman, 1998; Zachary, 2002).

New Directions for Adult and Continuing Education • DOI: 10.1002/ace

Kram (1985) states that mentors equally serve career development and psychosocial functions for the student. Daloz (1999) writes that mentors support, challenge, and provide vision for clientele. Cohen (1995), basing his model on Daloz's earlier work (1986), says that mentors function to (1) establish trust, (2) offer tailored advice, (3) introduce alternatives, (4) challenge, (5) motivate, and (6) encourage initiative. Jacobi (1991), in her review of the mentoring literature, adds that mentors show higher levels of experience and achievement and that the mentoring process is normally personal and reciprocal.

It is interesting to note how similar these functions are to traditional notions of effectively facilitating adults (Brookfield, 1986). Knox (1974) long ago equated mentoring with instruction or facilitating. "Persons who effectively serve as facilitators of learning," he wrote, "are able to perform well in the mentor role" (p. 18). Zachary (2002), however, disagrees. He says, "Being successful in the teacher role does not guarantee mentoring success; however, good teaching practice does inform good mentoring, and vice versa" (p. 37). Daloz (1999) sets mentors apart from "regular teachers" (p. 21), as he puts it, as they are more engaged and concerned with the individuality of their students.

This concern for the student as an individual is what seems to draw the line between teacher and mentor. Instructors as mentors are focused on the long-term development of the student rather than the short-term performance in the course. Online instructors can easily fall into the trap of losing sight of students' unique needs, particularly in asynchronous formats, where students' voices and personalities are reduced to lifeless text responses on a message board.

Mentoring Responsibilities of Instructors

The inclusion of mentoring as an instructional tool is vital in two key instances: when students are novices in online learning and when students have histories of marginalization and underrepresentation.

Supporting the Novice. Instructors need to recognize when students are new to the field and to the format and provide enough structure and direction to reduce their anxiety. Daloz (1999) and others recognize the value of such mentoring practices in the early stages of an online academic program. Returning or mature students often come to online learning formats with insecurities about their own technological and academic abilities, which are often situated within a constant reminder of their financial and family obligations (Knapper, as cited in Merriam, 1983). In addition, they are often unaccustomed to course designs and instructional delivery methods that require them to be autonomous, self-directed learners (Ascough, 2002; Johnson and Aragon, 2003). The sheer physical separateness between instructor and learner and between learners can lead an online learner to sense that he or she is not personally connected to the content (Rovai, 2002).

This is a particularly stressful phenomenon for students who are new to both the program and online learning. Equivalent to traveling to a foreign country with no preparation, these students are likely to be lacking in knowledge of the language, protocol, or survival tools that would help them to be successful. For many online students, the instructor serves as their only contact with the university; in essence, the instructor is the university. Students in these situations require that instructors serve as a trusted source in areas beyond the content of the course (Picciano, 2001).

Instructors should be involved in nurturing students from a sense of dependence to one of independence. Grow (1991) argues that an instructor's primary purpose is matching a student's current level of self-directedness and nurturing that student to higher stages. A lack of consideration for the fact that most adults have not been socialized to be independent, autonomous learners (Johnson and Aragon, 2003) leads to a situation where instructors focus more on the content of the course and the completion of course-related tasks instead of the development of the student from a dependent to an independent learner. The instructor works toward being eventually obsolete for his or her newly empowered students (Fassinger and Hensler-McGinnis, 2005).

There is a clear disconnect between novice students and self-disciplined, self-directed, and self-confident students whom Seeman (2001) describes as successful online students. Ascough (2002) says that students must significantly adjust their learning paradigms in order to be successful in this medium. Online learning often requires active, inquiry-focused learners; instructors should be focused on helping students with this role adjustment, which can often be a tense experience for them.

Supporting the Marginalized. Despite the false appearance of anonymity in the online environment, issues of race, gender, class, and sexual orientation remain factors in online student-student and instructor-student relationships (Fassinger and Hensler-McGinnis, 2005). Instructors who understand discrimination and oppression are in a better position to mentor students through the anticipated and encountered barriers to success (Hansman, 2000). Online instructors should recognize that many students bring with them histories of imposed silence and marginalization and legitimate those experiences by either addressing them in the content and delivery of the course or through personal interaction and counseling (Johnson-Bailey and Tisdell, 1998). However, Fassinger and Hensler-McGinnis (2005), in discussing a feminist, multicultural approach to mentoring, focus on the mentor's need to address issues of power and privilege with all mentees.

The real danger remains that online instructors may overlook underrepresented and marginalized groups for a couple of reasons. For one, the ethnic identity, social class, gender, or sexual orientation of online students is rarely evident. Instructors can encourage students to reveal more of themselves through personal pages, introduction threads on message boards, and assignments that require them to reflect on content through their own personal experiences. Instructors can use this information to discern whether students' backgrounds are affecting what they see.

Second, like their classroom counterparts, online instructors may be unaccustomed to working closely with students across cultural lines (Johnson-Bailey and Cervero, 2002). Instructors should, through critical reflection of their own practices, recognize their underlying assumptions about their students and put more effort into reaching out to any student, regardless of his or her societal status. Zachary (2000), as well as Johnson-Bailey and Cervero (2002), insist that mentors study the lives of their students to better understand their worldviews.

Incorporating Mentoring into Instructional Practice

For many online instructors, the acceptance of mentoring as an integral part of their instructional experience takes some getting used to. Many instructors are not well versed in adult development, adult learning styles, or the external lives of adults, or they may be socialized into traditional forms of instruction (Cho and Berge, 2002) and may feel it unnecessary and extremely difficult to mentor to students as individuals without interrupting the flow of the course (Zachary, 2002).

Several guidelines, used effectively, can help broaden the experience for even the most inexperienced online instructor.

Keep Your Eye on the Student. Instructors should seek and find students with whom to have more individual relationships. Perhaps a student is showing more confusion than the others do in his or her responses or seems to be overshadowed by more dominant voices. Perhaps a student shows exceptional promise but has not yet acknowledged his or her own potential. In a face-to-face environment, an instructor might talk with such a student after class, provide him or her with names of other contacts, suggest further reading, offer to meet with the student outside class hours, or offer to alter the requirements or expectations of the course based on a personal circumstance. The opportunity to pluck a student out of the crowd and take him or her under one's wing is often overlooked in online education.

Another way of addressing the student as individual is through active listening. Daloz (1999) describes "listening" as "actively engaging with the students' world and attempting to experience it from the inside" (p. 213). Instructors who mentor practice active listening, despite the digital medium. Active listening in a technical sense means (1) addressing students by name in their responses, (2) incorporating and celebrating their uniqueness as part of discussions, (3) avoiding cookie-cutter responses to their posts, and (4) recognizing which concerns should be addressed through private correspondence.

Provide Windows to the Future. Instructors should be opening new students to the possibilities of the future through modeling, reflection, and exposure to the greater academic and professional communities within which these beginning students wish to engage. For Daloz (1999), helping students to envision the future is one of the three main functions of a mentor (the others are supporting and challenging).

Model Revelation and Reflection. Instructors as mentors incorporate personal examples and experience as an integral part of the content. Daloz (1999) calls the openness of instructors to their students a "gift" for all parties that strengthens the mentor-student relationship (p. 214). Aragon (2003) says that the sharing of personal recollections and stories gives credibility to the instructor and allows students to see him or her as "human" (p. 65).

Expose Students to the Profession. Students should be conceptualizing the possible manifestations of their educational experience early on. Instructors can invite experts in the field to special chat sessions, or assign tasks that require students to explore and analyze the options available to them. Case studies involving situations they will most likely encounter in their professions, such as those exemplified in work by Smith (2005) on online collaborative learning groups, are a prime example. Instructors who are interested in mentoring should also incorporate their own research into classroom instruction as a means of giving context to the traditions, conventions, and culture of the profession (Marra and Pangborn, 2001.)

Invite Chaos When Appropriate. Daloz (1999) invites instructors to toss 'cow plops' on the road of truth"-that is, purposefully provoke thought, invite chaos when appropriate, and raise students' consciousness. In addition, instructors as mentors do not always answer the question or make decisions for the student (Johnson, Settimi, and Rogers, 2001; Smith, 2005).

Invite Others to Mentor. When there is a mix of experienced and inexperienced students in an online class, instructors can invite the more experienced peers to serve as mentors to the other students. Not only can they serve as additional levels of support and information for the instructor, but the peer mentors themselves are developing their own mentoring capacities. Many online programs employ graduate students or adjuncts to serve as mentors to online classes (Easton, 2000), freeing the instructor to concentrate fully on the content of the course.

Conclusion

Mentoring reminds the instructor that students are individuals who are at different learning stages, have differing goals and expectations, and have needs differing from those of their instructors. The kind of personal mentoring relationships described here may seem daunting, even overwhelming, when viewed under the bright light of grading, managing message boards, and leading chat sessions. But as Daloz (1999) argues, "if every teacher made a point of spending at least some real time with at least some students, our colleges and universities might be better places for genuine learning to occur" (p. 239).

Online instructors who choose to incorporate mentoring techniques into their practice are acknowledging that students deserve attention and nurturing both within and beyond the content. They show students that they are genuinely interested in their development as savvy online learners as well as professionals in the field.

References

Aragon, S. R. "Creating Social Presence in Online Environments." In S. R. Aragon (ed.), *Facilitating Learning in Online Environments. New Directions for Adult and Continuing Education*, no. 100. San Francisco: Jossey-Bass, 2003.

Ascough, R. S. "Designing for Online Distance Education: Putting Pedagogy Before Technology." *Teaching Theology and Religion*, 2002, 5(1), 17–29.

Brookfield, S. D. *Understanding and Facilitating Adult Learning.* San Francisco: Jossey-Bass, 1986.

Cafarella, R. S. *Psychosocial Development of Women.* Columbus, Ohio: ERIC Clearinghouse on Adult, Career and Vocational Education, 1993.

Cho, S. K., and Berge, Z. L. "Overcoming Barriers to Distance Training and Education." USDLA Journal, 2002, 16(1). Retrieved July 7, 2006, from http://www.usdla.org/html/journal/JAN02_Issue/article01.html.

Cohen, N. H. *Mentoring Adult Learners: A Guide for Educators and Trainers.* San Francisco: Jossey-Bass, 1995.

Collison, G., Elbaum, B., Haavind, S., and Tinker, R. *Facilitating Online Learning: Effective Strategies for Moderators.* Madison, Wis.: Atwood Publishing, 2000.

Daloz, L. A. *Effective Teaching and Mentoring: Realizing the Transformational Power of Adult Learning.* San Francisco: Jossey-Bass, 1986.

Daloz, L. A. *Mentor: Guiding the Journey of Adult Learners.* San Francisco: Jossey-Bass, 1999.

Easton, S. "Defining and Negotiating Roles in a Complex Virtual Organization: A Case Study of Instructors and Mentors in the Florida State University 2+2 Distance Learning Initiative." Unpublished doctoral dissertation, Florida State University, 2000.

English, L. M. "Spiritual Dimensions of Informal Learning." In L. M. English and M. A. Gillen (eds.), Addressing Spiritual Dimensions of Adult Learning. *New Directions for Adult and Continuing Education*, no. 85. San Francisco: Jossey-Bass, 2000.

Fassinger, R. E., and Hensler-McGinnis, N. F. "Multicultural Feminist Mentoring as Individual and Small-Group Pedagogy." In C. Z. Enns and A. L. Sinacore (eds.), Teaching and Social Justice. Washington, D.C.: American Psychological Association, 2005.

Grow, G. O. "Teaching Learners to Be Self-Directed." *Adult Education Quarterly*, 1991, 41(3), 125–149.

Hansman, C. A. "Mentoring and Women's Career Development." In L. L. Bierema (ed.), Women's Career Development Across the Lifespan: Insights and Strategies for Women, Organizations, and Adult Educators. *New Directions for Adult and Continuing Education*, no. 80. San Francisco: Jossey-Bass, 1998.

Hansman, C. "Formal Mentoring Programs." In A. Wilson and E. Hayes (eds.), *Handbook of Adult and Continuing Education*. (New ed.) San Francisco: Jossey-Bass, 2000.

Hiemstra, R., and Brockett, R. G. "From Mentor to Partner: Lessons from a Personal Journey." In I. M. Saltiel, A. Sgroi, and R. G. Brockett (eds.), The Power and Potential of Collaborative Learning Partnerships. *New Directions for Adult and Continuing Education*, no. 79. San Francisco: Jossey-Bass, 1998.

Jacobi, M. "Mentoring and Undergraduate Academic Success: A Literature Review." *Review of Educational Research*, 1991, *61*(4), 505–532.

Johnson, S. D., and Aragon, S. R. "An Instructional Strategy Framework for Online Learning Environments." In S. R. Aragon (ed.), Facilitating Learning in Online Environments. *New Directions for Adult and Continuing Education*, no. 100. San Francisco: Jossey-Bass, 2003.

Johnson, T.R.B., Settimi, P. D., and Rogers, J. L. "Mentoring in the Health Professions." In A. G. Reinarz and E. R. White (eds.), Beyond Teaching to Mentoring. *New Directions for Teaching and Learning*, no. 85. San Francisco: Jossey-Bass, 2001.

Johnson-Bailey, J., and Cervero, R. M. "Cross-Cultural Mentoring as a Context for Learning." In J. Johnson-Bailey and R. M. Cervero (eds.), *Cross-Cultural Mentoring as a Context for Learning*. New Directions for Adult and Continuing Education, no. 96. San Francisco: Jossey-Bass, 2002.

Johnson-Bailey, J., and Tisdell, E. J. "Diversity Issues in Women's Career Development." In L. L. Bierema (ed.), Women's Career Development Across the Lifespan: Insights and Strategies for Women, Organizations, and Adult Educators. *New Directions for Adult and Continuing Education*, no. 80. San Francisco: Jossey-Bass, 1998.

Knox, A. B. "Higher Education and Lifelong Learning." *Journal of Research and Development in Education*, 1974, 7(4), 13–17.

Kram, K. E. "Phases of the Mentor Relationship." *Academy of Management Journal*, 1985, 26(4), 608–625.

Levinson, D. J., and others. The Seasons of a Man's Life. New York: Knopf, 1978.

Marra, R. M., and Pangborn, R. N. "Mentoring in the Technical Disciplines: Fostering a Broader View of Education, Career, and Culture in and Beyond the Workplace." In A. G. Reinarz and E. R. White (eds.), *Beyond Teaching to Mentoring*. New Directions for Teaching and Learning, no. 85. San Francisco: Jossey-Bass, 2001.

Merriam, S. "*Mentors and Protégés: A Critical Review of the Literature*." Adult Education Quarterly, 1983, 33(3), 161–173.

Picciano, A. G. *Distance Learning: Making Connections Across Virtual Space and Time*. Upper Saddle River, N.J.: Prentice Hall/Merrill, 2001.

Rovai, A. P. "Building Sense of Community at a Distance." *International Review of Research in Open and Distance Learning*, 2002, 3. Retrieved July 7, 2006, from http://www.irrodl.org/index.php/irrodl/article/view/79/152.

Seeman, E. "Creating an Online Orientation and Student Support Services." In C. Dalziel and M. Payne (eds.), *Quality Enhancing Practices in Distance Education: Student Services*. Washington, D.C.: Instructional Telecommunications Council, 2001.

Smith, R. O. "Working with Difference in Online Collaborative Groups." *Adult Education Quarterly*, 2005, 55(3), 182–199.

Zachary, L. J. *The Mentor's Guide: Facilitating Effective Learning Relationships*. San Francisco: Jossey-Bass, 2000.

Zachary, L. J. "The Role of Teacher as Mentor." In J. Ross-Gordon (ed.), *Contemporary Viewpoints on Teaching Adults Effectively*. New Directions for Adult and Continuing Education, no. 93. San Francisco: Jossey-Bass, 2002.

KIMBERLY R. BURGESS *is a faculty mentor of elementary education preservice teachers at Western Governors University.*

New Directions for Adult and Continuing Education • DOI: 10.1002/ace

6

This chapter looks at the development and nature of learning objects, meta-tagging standards and taxonomies, learning object repositories, learning object repository characteristics, and types of learning object repositories, with type examples.

Learning Object Repositories

Rosemary Lehman

During the past few years, a new way of thinking, object-oriented thinking, has spawned the creation of small, reusable educational chunks of digital information that educators and trainers can archive and use in their course building and also share with others. Archiving and sharing eliminates the need to recreate what has already been produced, stimulates collaboration and ingenuity, and can provide rich support for learning. This thinking and creating are increasingly taking hold across the social sector in education, government, and business. These digital chunks of information take on many forms: text, video, audio, graphics, and multimedia and include tutorials, scenarios, simulations, lesson modules, case studies, and assessments. The accepted term for these small units of learning is learning objects. To enable their accessibility, reusability, generativity, shareability, durability, and scalability, meta-tagging standards and learning object repositories are evolving.

A Closer Look at Learning Objects

More than thirty years ago, Gerard (2006) suggested that curriculum units in computer-based instruction could be made smaller and combined in various ways for customization and use by individual learners. Learning objects are an application of this type of object-oriented thinking, and during the past few years, they have drawn the attention of education, government, and business. Multiple definitions have evolved to describe learning objects. The definition that is now most widely accepted is that of Wiley (2000): "any digital resource that can be reused to support learning" (p. 7) and can be used in multiple contexts.

NEW DIRECTIONS FOR ADULT AND CONTINUING EDUCATION, no. 113, Spring 2007 © 2007 Wiley Periodicals, Inc.
Published online in Wiley InterScience (www.interscience.wiley.com) • DOI: 10.1002/ace.247

Wiley (2000) has also created a taxonomy that specifies different kinds of learning objects. The types are differentiated by "the manner in which the object to be classified exhibits certain characteristics" (p. 22). These characteristics apply across environments and include the number of combined elements, categories of objects contained, reusable components, common functions, extra-object dependence, type of log-in contained in the object, and the potential for both inter- and intracontextual reuse. Additional descriptions of learning objects incorporate six key characteristics: accessibility, interoperability, adaptability, reusability, durability, and granularity ("Learning Object Authoring Zone Networks," 2004).

Shepherd (2006) views learning objects as serving a variety of purposes and suggests three types, as shown in Table 6.1: integrated, informational, and practice and review. For example, an instructor could develop a physics simulation that would include supportive information (integrated), create a descriptive instructional design model (informational), or create a course review exercise (practice and review).

Learning Objects: Meta-Tagging Standards and Taxonomies

The use of learning objects necessitates employing meta-tags for ease of search, retrieval, and use. Meta-tagging is "data about data" and needs to be thoughtfully determined and selected by instructors and instructional

Table 6.1. Objects of Interest

Types of Learning Objects		
Integrated	Informational	Practice and Review
Mini-Tutorials	Overviews/summaries	Problems/case studies
Mini case studies, simulations, etc., with supportive information	Descriptions/definitions	Games/simulations
	Demonstrations/models	Drill-and-practice exercises
	Worked examples	Review exercises
	Cases/stories	Tests/assessments
	Papers/articles	
	Decision aids	

Source: Shepherd (2006).

designers and applied to the learning objects. These tags describe the content, their origin, form, applicability, and other significant characteristics.

Applying meta-tags to learning objects is the process of adding appropriate descriptions and values to the elements of the digital resources. The tags selected should match the main subject of the resource. The process used is to (1) decide what the resource is about, (2) select the appropriate terms that will help identify the resource, (3) enter the terms, and (4) make a final check of the tags. Appropriate tagging enables accessibility, interoperability, adaptability, reusability, durability, and scalability.

Both standards and taxonomies are critical to the development of meta-tags. Standards allow for interoperation, while taxonomies order, classify, and group according to presumed natural relationships, thus providing frameworks for discussion, analysis, or the retrieval of information. To facilitate the global adoption of learning object standards and taxonomies, a number of initiatives have emerged. The Dublin Core Metadata Initiative (2006) was created in 1965 to provide simple standards that would facilitate the finding, sharing, and management of information through describing resources, supporting a worldwide community of users and developers, and promoting widespread use of its solutions. The Learning Technology Standards Committee (LTSC) of the Institute of Electrical and Electronics Engineers (IEEE) was formed in 1996 ("ADL Background," 2006), and the Instructional Management Systems Project (2006) was developed several years later.

In 1997, the Department of Defense Advanced Distributed Learning (ADL) initiative was begun. Two years later, the first version of the Sharable Courseware Object Reference Model (SCORM) was drafted as the result of a perceived confusion and lack of coordination on the part of the earlier initiatives. The ADL SCORM focus became the integration and connection of the work of the other initiatives. In this effort, an attempt was made to adapt the Computer Managed Instruction model to the Internet, resulting in a Web-based communications model. ADL also worked closely with the IEEE and the Institute of Mathematical Statistics (IMS) to stabilize the metadata specification and create an XML binding. Later, ADL was able to realize an integration of the Aviation Industry CBT (Computer-Based Training) Committee (AICC) and IMS. This resulted in the IMS's content packaging specifications, which provide the functionality to describe and package learning materials, such as an individual course or a collection of courses into interoperable, distributable packages. Content packaging addresses the description, structure, and location of online learning materials and the definition of some particular content types ("Cover Pages by Oasis," 2006). AICC and IMS are now included in SCORM ("ADL Background," 2006).

An important aspect of using the learning objects is the organization, design, and search capabilities of the learning object in a specific format. For example, in the case of an American Sign Language (ASL) course (Conceição and Lehman, 2002), video-based learning objects were arranged in units and in categories that paralleled the course sequence. They were used for review and practice by the course learners. This arrangement was based on the instructional design of the course by the instructor and instructional designers. In other cases, learning objects may be organized differently, for example, around modules, themes, scenarios, critical incidents, or case studies. The use of search features helps users locate a specific topic, phrase, word, video, or graphic precisely when needed. A direct link to the learning object can also be incorporated. At London Metropolitan University, learning objects were used within online modules. The learning objects were created to help explain the complex aspects of Java programming. Text was complemented with multimedia to engage students visually. These learning objects were then integrated into course modules within the school's learning management system and introduced to the students for optional use. The learning objects were accessible using a direct link within the module (Bradley and Boyle, 2004).

With an increase in the number of learning objects being created and the development and refinement of meta-tagging standards and taxonomies, database-driven electronic spaces for accommodating the learning objects for retrieval and sharing have become necessary. The term used for these dynamic spaces is repositories.

Knowledge Repositories

Libraries and course management systems are considered knowledge repositories for large categories of information and course content. They have dealt mainly with archiving or the containing of information. Distinct access characteristics are usually required, as well as different log-ins. These knowledge repositories are structured in a variety of ways, making it difficult to exchange content in a flexible manner. In addition, they are conceived and designed as stand-alone systems instead of parts of a more cohesive resource of information. With the creation of smaller units for learning, that is, learning objects, the need for a different type of repository has emerged: learning object repositories.

Learning Object Repositories

Learning object repositories use well-researched user interfaces and architectures that make them easy to use, and they allow various levels of interactivity (Instructional Resource Center, 2006). Because the field of repositories is in its infancy, repository types and characteristics are only now beginning to be defined.

A learning object repository is an electronic database that accommodates a collection of small units of educational information or activities that can be accessed for retrieval and use. Learning object repositories enable the organization of learning objects, improve efficiencies, enhance learning object reuse and collaboration, and support learning opportunities. Repositories can consist of one database or several databases tied together by a common search engine. Organizations that operate digital repositories take on responsibility for the long-term maintenance of these digital resources, as well as for making the repositories available to communities agreed on by the depositor and the repository ("British Library," 2006).

One way of looking at learning object repositories is to divide them into three types: general, discipline specific, and commercial ("Learning Objects: Collections," 2003). Important factors to be taken into consideration when selecting the type of repository that will be most valuable is to look first at type match and then at the accessibility, flexibility, and usability for the end users: instructors, instructional designers, and learners.

Characteristics of Learning Object Repositories

As faculty interest in searching for preproduced case studies, out-of-class assignments, lab demonstrations, and extra credit work increases, the list of places vying to provide a home for learning objects is growing and providing users with an expanding number of choices (Long, 2004). In addition, projects and institutions are beginning to create their own customized repositories.

The successful selection or creation of a learning object repository depends on the specific characteristics that meet the needs of instructors, designers, and learners. Needs are the first and most important characteristic in this selection. Learning objects should be able to be easily accessed at the exact moment that the design need or learning activity calls for it. Content compatibility is another critical characteristic. Repositories created for specific topic areas or disciplines should be matched with that content. Other characteristics include the ease of the repository for sharing information with others, the capacity for collaboration, the capability for reuse of the learning objects, context sensitivity, coding and retrieval, editing, combining, and repurposing. Finally, there is the ease of accessibility for instructors and learners with diverse and special needs.

With the creation of learning objects and learning object repositories comes the need for answering the many questions that surface concerning digital rights and policy.

Learning Objects and Repositories: Digital Rights and Policy

When the Copyright Amendment Digital Agenda Act of 2000 came into effect, printed rights were broadened to include digital rights. These rights promote creative endeavors while allowing reasonable access to copyright material.

New Directions for Adult and Continuing Education • DOI: 10.1002/ace

They include the right to make materials available online, as well as the right to transmit works electronically. It is important to know that rights are not limited to a specific technology.

Digital rights have a heavy impact on the academic world and other types of education and training. Educational and training institutions need to manage their use of intellectual property to ensure they are complying with the law. As a result of the new Digital Agenda reforms, educational organizations must become far more vigilant about ways in which teaching staff use and manage protected intellectual property. All teachers and educational managers need to recognize they have an obligation to understand the implications of their work in relation to using the copyright-protected materials of other persons (Australian Flexible Learning Framework, 2006).

Digital rights management (DRM) standardization is now occurring in a number of open organizations. The solutions to these challenges will enable large amounts of new content to be made available in open, safe, and trusted environments. Industry and users are now demanding that standards be developed to allow interoperability. By doing this, content owners and managers would not be forced to encode their works in proprietary formats or systems. DRM architecture is fundamental to interoperability and openness. It includes Internet protocol (IP) asset creation capture (rights validation, creation, and work flow), IP asset management (repository, content and metadata, trading, payments, and packaging), and IP asset use (permission and tracking) (Iannella, 2001).

Learning Object Repositories: Some Lists and Examples

One way to look at learning object repositories is to divide them into three types: general, discipline specific, and commercial ("Learning Objects Repositories," 2006). A number of lists and charts have been developed that include repositories of these types. Among them are the "Academic ADL Directory of Learning Object Repositories Listing" (2006), the "Learning Object Collections" (2006), and the "Learning Objects Repositories" (2006).

General Repositories. Following are examples of general learning object repositories:

• CLOE: Cooperative Learning Object Exchange, http://cloe.on.ca/. CLOE was founded at the University of Waterloo and currently consists of seventeen university partners in Ontario. Of significance is that CLOE attempts to foster a collaborative model for the development, use, and reuse of learning objects. Fundamental to this is the creation of a virtual market economy whereby virtual credits are awarded for objects that are used and reused the most. Those who wish to use the services of CLOE must register.

• European Knowledge Pool System (ARIADNE), http://www.ariadne-eu.org/. ARIADNE is a European association open to the world for the sharing of knowledge and its reuse. It was developed to deliver educational content throughout Europe and facilitate the sharing and reuse of educational resources. This encouragement of the discovery and reuse of these materials promotes an increasing recognition that learning object production is a valid field of activity for academics. The collection contains materials of a wide variety of interactivity levels in many European languages, primarily English, French, Italian, German, and Dutch. ARIADNE has four levels of access: (1) open to everyone through a default account, (2) members only, (3) registered users of the server on which the material was uploaded, and (4) only after contact with the rights holder.

• Wisconsin Online Resource Center Wisc-Online Learning Object Project, http://www.wisc-online.com/. Wisc-Online is an international award-winning learning object repository that contains over two thousand learning objects, with new ones continuously under development. Although it was developed primarily by faculty from the Wisconsin Technical College System (WTCS), produced by multimedia technicians, and made available at no cost and with copyright clearance for use in any WTCS classroom or online application, it can be used by other colleges, universities, and consortia around the world, with permission. Users click to sign on and receive a password. Current use of the learning object repository exceeds twenty thousand hits per day. The process used to develop the learning object repository is described in Chitwood, May, Bunnow, and Langan (2000).

• Multimedia Educational Resource for Learning and Online Teaching (MERLOT), http://www.merlot.org/Home.po. MERLOT is often referred to as both a repository and "referatory." It is a free and open resource designed primarily for faculty and students of higher education. Links to online learning materials are collected here, along with annotations such as peer reviews and assignments. The MERLOT community is made up of individual members, higher education, institutions, and corporate partners and affiliates dedicated to improving education. Individual MERLOT members support the community by contributing materials and adding assignments and comments to the MERLOT collection. MERLOT partners contribute infrastructure, guidance, and expertise.

Discipline Specific. Following are examples of discipline-specific learning object repositories:

• Global Education Online Depository and Exchange (GEODE), http://www.uw-igs.org/. This repository provides networking, funding, and developmental opportunities to University of Wisconsin campuses interested in increasing interdisciplinary cooperation and scholarship around global issues. It was created in 1999 in response to the commissioned Wisconsin International Trade Council's Report that identified a need for greater international literacy among members of the Wisconsin workforce. The repository is maintained by the University of Wisconsin System's Institute for Global Studies and permits queries by country, region, file format, language, or keyword. No registration is required for this repository.

• Health Education Assets Library (HEAL), http://www.healcentral .org. Conceived in 1998 and having begun its collection development in 2002, this repository provides building-block multimedia items (images, videos, and animations), as well as textual materials like case studies and quizzes. Its current prototype collection of over a thousand materials contains resources useful to medical students and medical professionals. The collection will eventually contain materials of use to all educational levels. It currently contains images and interactive tutorials. This site is freely accessible to everyone. Registration is not necessary.

• Math Forum, http://mathforum.org. One of the oldest collections of learning materials on the Internet, the Math Forum is a leading electronic center for mathematics and mathematics education. The Math Forum is a learning repository for both interactive and text-based materials, as well as a site for mathematics educators and learners to engage in person-to-person interactions and discuss and exchange educational products and services. The Math Forum encourages the exchange of educational materials by facilitating dialogue and connections among educators. This repository is freely searchable but also offers math problem packages for purchase.

• American Sign Language, http://www.uwex.edu/ics/learningobjects/. This customized repository is password-protected, along with the need to e-mail the owners for purposes of tracking. The repository is part of a University of Wisconsin-Milwaukee and University of Wisconsin-Extension American Sign Language (ASL) Learning Objects Project. This repository contains video-based ASL learning objects, in individual words and phrases, performed by a native ASL speaker. These video-based learning objects have been created in a variety of delivery formats. They are currently being tested for effectiveness of use on CD-ROMs in ASL classes. Their use is also being tested on handheld computers and in this knowledge repository. It is recommended that these ASL video-based learning objects be used as an instructional aid in combination with an ASL program or course. RealPlayer is needed to play the videos (Conceição and Lehman, 2002). The learning objects for the knowledge repository have been meta-tagged for SCORM compliance and recategorized for easy access by the general public. The opening page of the repository provides an example of a learning object to introduce the users to the format of the individual signs. It then directs users to the appropriate signs.

Commercial/Hybrid. Following is an example of commercial/hybrid learning object repositories:

- XanEdu, http://xanedu.com/. XanEdu provides faculty with the resources necessary for gathering and delivering information and provides instructors and instructional designers. Other trends must include increased repository sustainability, better funding, more clearly stated educational goals for repository infrastructure, an expanding number of repositories that will eventually reach a critical mass, instructor and learner repository orientation, and instructor and learner training for the more sophisticated creation and use of learning objects and learning object repositories.

References

"Academic ADL Directory of Learning Object Repositories Listing." Retrieved Jan. 12, 2006, from http://projects.aadlcolab.org/repositorydirectory/repository_listing.asp.

"ADL Background." Retrieved Jan. 14, 2006, from http://www.rhassociates.com/adl_background.htm.

"Australian Flexible Learning Framework." Retrieved Jan. 14, 2006, from http://www.flexiblelearning.net.au/leaders/fl_leaders/fll02/finalreport/final_hand_higgs_meredith.pdf.

Bradley, C., and Boyle, T. "Students' Use of Learning Objects." Interactive Multimedia Electronic Journal of Computer-Enhanced Learning, 2004, 6(2). Retrieved Oct. 12, 2006, from http://imej.wfu.edu/articles/2004/2/01/index.asp.

"British Library." Retrieved Jan. 6, 2006, from http://www.bl.uk/about/strategic/glossary.html.

Chitwood, K., May, C., Bunnow, D., and Langan, T. "Battle Stories from the Field: Wisconsin Online Resource Center Learning Objects Project." In D. A. Wiley (ed.), The Instructional Use of Learning Objects: Online Version. 2000. Retrieved May 18, 2001, from http://reusability.org/read/chapters/chitwood.doc.

Conceição, S., and Lehman, R. "Creating Learning Objects to Enhance the Educational Experiences of American Sign Language Learners: An Instructional Development Report." Canadian Journal of Learning and Technology, 2002, 28(3), 91–103.

Conceição, S., Olgren, C., and Ploetz, P. "Reusing Learning Objects in Three Settings: Implications for Online Instruction." International Journal of Instructional Technology and Distance Learning, 2006, 3(4). Retrieved Oct. 14, 2006, from http://www.itdl.org/ Journal/April_06/article01.htm.

Cover Pages by Oasis. Retrieved Feb. 18, 2006, from http://xml.coverpages.org/ni2001-05-08-a.html.

"Dublin Core Metadata Initiative." Retrieved Jan. 14, 2006, from http://dublincore.org/about/.

Gerard, R. W. "Shaping the Mind: Computers in Education." In R. C. Atkinson and H. A. Wilson (eds.), Computer-Assisted Instruction: A Book of Readings. Orlando, Fla.: Academic Press, Health Education Assets Library, 2006. Retrieved Jan. 25, 2006, from http://www.healcentral.org/.

Iannella, R. "Digital Rights Management (DRM) Architectures." D-Lib Magazine, 2001, 7(6). Retrieved Jan. 25, 2006, from http://www.dlib.org/dlib/june01/iannella/06iannella.html.

"Instructional Management Systems Project." Retrieved Jan. 14, 2006, from http://www. imsglobal.org/.
Instructional Resource Center. Teaching with Technology: Introduction to Learning Object Repositories. Retrieved Jan. 5, 2006, from http://www.irc.gmu.edu/resources/ findingaid/twt_guides/repos.htm.
"Learning Object Authoring Zone Networks." Retrieved Nov. 22, 2004, from http://www.loaz.com/learning-objects/learning-object-characteristics.html.
"Learning Objects: Collections." Retrieved Jan. 25, 2006, from http://www.uwm.edu/Dept/CIE/AOP/LO_collections.htm.
"Learning Objects Repositories." Retrieved Jan. 8, 2006, from http://72.14.203.104/u/UTSAEDU?q=cache:IOoNHG81VXMJ:elearning.utsa.edu/guides/LOrepositories.htm+Learning+Objects+Repositories&hl=en&gl=us&ct=clnk&cd=1&ie=UTF-8.
Long, P. D. "Learning Object Repositories, Digital Repositories, and the Reusable Life of Course Content." *Campus Technology Magazine,* 2004. Retrieved Mar. 16, 2006, from http://www.campus-technology.com/print.asp?ID=9258.
Shepherd, C. *Objects of Interest.* Retrieved Jan. 12, 2006, from http://www.fastrak-consulting.co.uk/tactix/features/objects/objects.htm.
University of Wisconsin Institute for Global Studies. Retrieved Jan. 24, 2006, from http://www.uw-igs.org/.
Wiley, D. A. "Connecting Learning Objects to Instructional Design Theory: A Definition, a Metaphor, and a Taxonomy." In D. A. Wiley (ed.), *The Instructional Use of Learning Objects: Online Version.* 2000. Retrieved Jan. 5, 2006, from http://reusability.org/read/chapters/wiley.doc.
Wisc-Online Resource Center. Retrieved Feb. 12, 2006, from www.wisc-online.com/

ROSEMARY LEHMAN *is senior outreach/distance education specialist at Instructional Communications Systems, University of Wisconsin-Extension, and manager of the Instructional Communications Systems instructional design team.*

New Directions for Adult and Continuing Education • DOI: 10.1002/ace

7

Discussion boards have the unique capacity to support higher-order constructivist learning and the development of a learning community, This chapter provides ten conditions that support the effective use of an online discussion.

The Online Discussion Board

S. Joseph Levine

> Teaching by discussion differs from lecturing because you never know what is going to happen. At times this is anxiety-producing, at times frustrating, but more often exhilarating. It provides constant challenges and opportunities for both you and the students to learn.
> —W. J. McKeachie (2002, p. 51)

The online discussion board has become a ubiquitous part of today's distance learning landscape. Wherever you look, you will find a discussion board. Discussion boards have become the central element in every classroom management system that extends teaching beyond the traditional campus classroom. With this quick rise in popularity and use, however, comes another challenge: the effective use of this potentially powerful instructional element. According to Garrison and Anderson (2003), "the educational community has barely begun to appreciate the collaborative capabilities of e-learning and, as a result, these capabilities are greatly underutilized" (p. 22).

The assumption is often made that the online discussion board can serve to provide and substitute for the interactive dimensions found in the face-to-face classroom. Although learners may be separated by time or place, it is usually assumed that the online discussion board can connect learners and teachers in ways similar to the natural interpersonal relationships associated with being in a room together. In this chapter, however, I put forth a different assumption: that the online discussion board provides a unique potential that is not automatically present in a face-to-face situation. This unique potential is based on the capacity of the online discussion board to

NEW DIRECTIONS FOR ADULT AND CONTINUING EDUCATION, no. 113, Spring 2007 © 2007 Wiley Periodicals, Inc.
Published online in Wiley InterScience (www.interscience.wiley.com) • DOI: 10.1002/ace.248

support higher-order constructivist learning and the development of a learning community. Palloff and Pratt (2005) define constructivism as a process of learning that "is active and is involved with constructing rather than acquiring knowledge"(p. 6). Learners are able to build understandings by interacting with their world. Weller (2002) says that constructivism is a popular approach with online courses, and "a course that adopts some element of constructivism will incorporate structured discussion" (p. 65). Palloff and Pratt (1999) point out that it is through the various interactions that can be accommodated through an online discussion board that a constructivistic approach is facilitated leading to successful learning. Garrison and Anderson (2003) push the idea of the unique or distinctive potential of online discussion, and the challenge facing the online educator to capitalize on this uniqueness, when they state, "Discourse goes to the core of the e-learning experience in that interaction is where the strength of e-learning lies and is the essence of an educational experience as evidenced by a collaborative inquiry-based process. Facilitation of the learning experience is the greatest challenge facing teachers in an e-learning environment" (pp. 83–84).

The discussion board has the potential to provide the basis for creating a climate whereby the learning process is not limited by the traditions of face-to-face instruction.

Conditions Supporting an Online Discussion Board

The literature regarding online learning is growing at a remarkable rate, and as each piece of literature is examined, it becomes evident that the online discussion board plays a key role in making the educational experience both powerful and dynamic. Tu and McIsaac (2002) suggest that asynchronous learning can be helpful to students who have fewer keyboarding skills but caution that students can feel lost in a multithreaded discussion environment. Vrasidas and McIsaac (1999) remind us that "when students do not receive feedback, they do not continue to post messages. Unless students receive immediate feedback, they feel they are posting to the network without any response" (p. 33). Ko and Rossen (2001) caution that it is important to create appropriate guidelines and procedures in advance to guarantee the discussion is focused. And Burkett, Leard, and Spector (2004) refer to "just-in-time learning," whereby the instructor can "add relevant information to a discussion when and where it is needed" (p. 7). This can allow the instructor to respond to teachable moments.

The challenge for online educators is to organize the countless suggestions into a meaningful list that can serve as a guide for facilitating interaction in a discussion board. The following ten conditions that support the effective use of an online discussion board are provided as an initial basis for such a guide.

Condition 1: Create an Environment Conducive to Learning. Knowles (1980), in writing about andragogy, describes the need to establish at the beginning of a course a climate that is truly conducive to learning. Although his frame of reference is face-to-face instruction, his concerns about the physical environment and the psychological environment have direct implications for online discussion boards. Knowles posits that the instructional climate be established so that it functions well as a place for learning. He suggests that "the social climate of an activity is affected by everything that happens during the course of the activity, but at no time with the potency of the impact of the opening session" (p. 226). Smith (2005) relates these concerns to the online environment when she describes specific steps that help learners feel comfortable interacting with each other online: "The process of warming up and forming the learning community can include a mix of synchronous and asynchronous communication. The goals should be that learners: 1) get to know one another and build relationships, 2) develop comfort with the technology, practicing the skills of online communication and conversation, 3) safely practice revealing themselves, and 4) reflect on their learning possibilities in this environment" (p. 101).

Condition 2: Establish Rules, and Provide Introductory Instruction. The advent of computer technology to support instruction has been rather startling. It has come on us quickly, and it has reinforced the need to carefully and methodically introduce students to the technology and how the technology will be used. The online discussion board does not enjoy the power of immediate nonverbal feedback that is often a key to the effectiveness of a face-to-face class. It is essential to establish initial ground rules, take time in delivering instructions so that learners will not get lost, and clarify exactly what will be expected during the course. As teachers become more familiar with the technology, they tend to take more for granted. The omission of a meaningful introduction to a discussion board and the lack of clarified rules for interacting can have a debilitating effect on interaction and learning. Chute, Thompson, and Hancock (1999) state that "the instructor needs to set the stage for the distance learning program in the first 20 minutes of the initial session" (p. 133). Palloff and Pratt (2005) suggest a number of questions that need to be answered in order to establish a viable environment that can support a discussion board—for instance, How long should online interactions last? Must all activity take place on the discussion board? Is there a space where groups can meet privately? Is it possible to use telephone calls and other forms of synchronous communication? Will face-to-face sessions be encouraged? Comeaux (2002) sums it up nicely when she says that "in contrast to collaboration activities in face-to-face classes, online collaborative tasks should be structured enough to diminish student confusion" (p. 187).

Condition 3: Guide the Threaded Discussion. The first discussion boards were linear in nature: messages were presented in sequence based on the time in which they were posted. The discussion board took on the appearance of a very long page, with one posting following another, regardless of the topic of the posting. This made it difficult for learners to connect messages that dealt with the same topic. It created considerable work for them if they wanted to follow the progression of thinking that surrounded an idea or thread. The threaded discussion format resolves this problem since it includes topics and subtopics that allow the systematic organization of the discussion by the learners themselves as the discussion progresses. It provides the learners and teacher with a number of threads or side conversations in which to participate. In a threaded discussion, learners can respond to comments at any time in an online conversation and have their comments placed within the thread to which they are responding. It is essential that the teacher establish meaningful discussion threads at the beginning of a course, organize topics and subtopics, construct postings that serve to reinforce the focus of a thread when the thread appears to be wandering off topic, provide feedback to learner postings, and redirect and reinforce as needed.

Condition 4: Pose Meaningful Questions and Problems. In the dynamic milieu of an online discussion board where learning is a function of knowledge construction rather than just acquiring information, the teacher must move beyond asking questions and be able to pose problems in question form for the learners to consider. Paulo Freire (1973) differentiates between the teacher's role in asking questions and the role in posing questions or problems when he says that those truly committed to a liberating form of education "must abandon the educational goal of deposit-making and replace it with the posing of the problems of men in their relations with the world" (p. 66). If we consider the online discussion board as a vehicle for dialogical relations, we can then understand Freire's suggestion of the role of the teacher as a problem-posing educator constantly reforming his reflections in the reflection of the students. The students are no longer docile listeners but co-investigators in dialogue with the teacher.

Condition 5: Focus on the Highest Three Levels of the Cognitive Domain. According to Bloom and others (1956), the lowest two levels of the cognitive domain—knowledge and comprehension—are based on a didactic approach to teaching that is focused on the delivery of information. The third level of the domain, application, is concerned with facilitating learning by putting information and understanding to use. It is at the highest three levels of the cognitive domain—analysis, synthesis, and evaluation—that learning is achieved through a process of interaction and dialogue. And it is at these higher levels of the cognitive domain that an online discussion board can best assist learning. Waterhouse (2005) states, "Electronic discussions are one of the most powerful components of elearn ing, especially when they are designed to promote critical thinking, active learning, and the higher levels of Bloom's Taxonomy" (p. 120). The highest levels of the cognitive domain are built around the assumption that all ideas, regardless of whether they are presented by the teacher or the learners, are important and valued. And it is through discussion that concepts are challenged and new ideas are generated. Encouraging learners to analyze, synthesize, and draw value judgments is an appropriate and essential use of the discussion board.

Condition 6: Allow Individualization Without Isolation. Certainly online instruction appeals to many learners because of the opportunity to participate in a very individual manner that is guided by the learner's own schedule and time demands. However, the effect of this power to control participation can lead the learner to a sense of isolation. And as more and more learners in an online course become isolated, the course can lose its dynamic instructional power and appear more like a set of learning materials sitting idly on an electronic shelf. It is crucial that the online educator effectively deal with this negative aspect of individualization and replace it with a recognition of the learner as a unique individual—a valued participant in the online learning activity. The reinforcing of unique and individual personalities can be encouraged by providing an opportunity for participant introductions at the beginning of a course, referring to specific learners by name, crediting specific learners when their ideas are described and shared with the group, building on the ideas presented by members of the group, and providing affirming feedback when important contributions are made to the discussion.

Condition 7: Be Sensitive to Nonparticipation. The best way to deal with nonparticipation is by creating a learning environment that strongly encourages participation. Indications of nonparticipation can go unnoticed for quite some time. And yet a student who is not very active in posting comments to the discussion board may be highly involved in what is going on. According to Comeaux (2002), "In our experience, many students were frequent readers and less frequent posters. Some of the best comments came from students who read often, then replied with insight gained from hearing the others out before responding" (p. 223). When it becomes apparent that a particular learner is not participating, it may be too late to bring about change. Using e-mail to communicate directly and personally with specific learners can help the instructor better understand whether a student is really participating. Two-way e-mail conversations that connect the teacher with individual learners can be a highly effective way to energize participation in an online discussion board.

Condition 8: Stimulate Participation. Encouraging learners to participate actively in an online discussion board can be a major challenge. Without being able to see the learners, it can be difficult to know who is or who is not participating—or, more important, who is or is not learning.

Gilly Salmon (2000) provides excellent guidance to the online teacher through her five-stage model of participation in computer-mediated conferencing. Each step in the model requires the learner to master certain technical skills and the teacher to provide different e-moderating skills. Stage One occurs prior to the first posting of a message and is concerned with access and motivation. Stage Two is concerned with online socialization and networking. Stage Three is concerned with initiating information exchange and is often accompanied by large numbers of messages on the discussion board. In Stage Four, knowledge construction, learners begin to interact more substantively with each other. The fifth and final stage is that of development. At this time, learners become more responsible for their own learning and need less and less support from the teacher. The focus becomes constructivist in nature, where exploration and knowledge building are important. The view of the teacher as a provider of information diminishes.

Condition 9: Encourage Reflection. Since the online discussion board operates in an asynchronous mode, with teacher and learners involved at times most convenient to each, there can be time to process ideas and concepts and reflect on meaning. Anderson and Garrison (1998) underscore the essential and powerful role that reflection plays in an online discussion board when they state, "The capacity to support interaction in an asynchronous format provides an opportunity for reflection and deliberation not found in any synchronous learning environment—including face-to-face classrooms" (p. 103). Reflection, of course, does not necessarily occur without some degree of encouragement. To help in the reflection process, it is very important to provide discussion questions and challenges that encourage reflection. Levine (2005) describes this essential instructor role in the online environment and states, "To actually energize the interaction, the instructor must search out ways to unobtrusively encourage learners to share their experience, knowledge, and willingness to help each other. When the instructor is able to accomplish this form of learner encouragement, learner-learner relationships will develop and form a powerful foundation for the instruction" (p. 21).

Condition 10: Summarize Key Ideas. One of the beneficial qualities of the online discussion board is that all postings are available to be read, reacted to, and reflected on throughout the length of the course. This archiving feature, though potentially powerful, needs the assistance of the instructor to be truly viable, especially when a constructivist approach is followed. According to Eastmond (1995), "There is nothing inherent in computer conferencing to cause reflection. Yet, it presents many of the necessary elements: a group inquiry environment that invites analysis and synthesis of readings, opinions, and experiences, without limits to the amount of feedback the learner can give or receive. Given skillful moderation toward facilitating reflection, it will likely occur" (p. 88). The challenge for the instructor is to provide the framework by which each learner individually summarizes his or her own learnings that have accrued from the online discussion board and reflects on the meaning. The instructor needs to ask a series of three questions based on "what," "why," and "now what." The what question is designed to have the learner reflect back on the discussion in terms of what key ideas (what new concepts, what unanswered questions, what additional concerns, and so forth) were brought about through a particular thread or focus during the discussion. For each point that a learner identifies, he or she is then asked the why question: to analyze why the key idea is important, the unique meaning it has, or the way in which he or she has been affected by it. Learners are encouraged to move back and forth between the what and why questions as they examine the importance of the discussion for them. Finally, learners are challenged to generalize with the now what question and move from the discussion board to their own world. This model for debriefing provides not only a systematic way for summarizing but also helps move the learning beyond the discussion board and into the world of each learner.

Implications for Adult Learners

Not seen as merely a tool to make online learning "as good as" in-person education, the online discussion board presents unique opportunities for teaching in new ways. Building on a constructivist view of learning, it can stimulate an individualized form of learning at the higher levels of the cognitive domain. It can provide learners with exceptional opportunities for self-expression and reflection. According to Weller (2002), "The more didactic pedagogy of face-to-face lecturing does not translate well onto the Net, and so an approach that places less emphasis on the educator and more on the learner, and that positively encourages communication, seems to offer an alternative that makes the online course a distinct, and perhaps more attractive, offering" (p. 65).

References

Anderson, T., and Garrison, R. D. "Learning in a Networked World: New Roles and Responsibilities." In C. C. Gibson (ed.), *Distance Learners in Higher Education*. Madison, Wis.: Atwood Publishing, 1998.

Bloom, B., and others. Taxonomy of Educational Objectives: The Classification of Educational Goals. *Handbook I: Cognitive Domain*. New York: Longman, Green, 1956.

Burkett, R. S., Leard, C., and Spector, B. S. "Using an Electronic Bulletin Board in Science Teacher Education: Issues and Trade-Offs." *Journal of Interactive Online Learning*, 2004, 3(1). Retrieved July 6, 2006, from http://www.ncolr.org/jiol/issues/PDF/3.1.1.pdf.

Chute, A. G., Thompson, M. M., and Hancock, B. W. *The McGraw-Hill Handbook of Distance Learning*. New York: McGraw-Hill, 1999.

Comeaux, P. *Communication and Collaboration in the Online Classroom: Examples and Applications*. Bolton, Mass.: Anker Publishing Company, 2002.

Eastmond, D. V. *Alone But Together: Adult Distance Study Through Computer Conferencing*. Cresskill, N.J.: Hampton Press, 1995.

Freire, P. *Pedagogy of the Oppressed*. New York: Seabury Press, 1973.

Garrison, D. R., and Anderson, T. *E-Learning in the 21st Century*. London: Routledge Falmer, 2003.

Knowles, M. S. *The Modern Practice of Adult Education: From Pedagogy to Andragogy*. Chicago: Follett, 1980.

Ko, S., and Rossen, S. *Teaching Online: A Practical Guide*. Boston: Houghton Mifflin, 2001.

Levine, S. J. "Creating a Foundation for Learning Relationships." In S. J. Levine (ed.), *Making Distance Education Work: Understanding Learning and Learners at a Distance*. Okemos, Mich.: LearnerAssociates.net, 2005.

McKeachie, W. J. *McKeachie's Teaching Tips: Strategies, Research, and Theory for College and University Teachers*. (11th ed.) Boston: Houghton Mifflin, 2002.

Palloff, R. M., and Pratt, K. *Building Learning Communities in Cyberspace*. San Francisco: Jossey-Bass, 1999.

Palloff, R. M., and Pratt, K. *Collaborating Online: Learning Together in Community*. San Francisco: Jossey-Bass, 2005.

Salmon, G. *E-Moderating: The Key to Teaching and Learning Online*. London: Kogan Page, 2000.

Smith, L. "Promoting Learner-to-Learner Interaction in Online Distance Education." In S. J. Levine (ed.), *Making Distance Education Work: Understanding Learning and Learners at a Distance*. Okemos, Mich.: LearnerAssociates.net, 2005.

Tu, C., and McIsaac, M. "The Relationship of Social Presence and Interaction in Online Classes." *American Journal of Distance Education*, 2002, *16*(3), 131–150.

Vrasidas, C., and McIsaac, M. S. "Factors Influencing Interaction in an Online Course." *American Journal of Distance Education*, 1999, *13*(3), 22–26.

Waterhouse, S. *The Power of eLearning: The Essential Guide for Teaching in the Digital Age*. Boston: Pearson Education, 2005.

Weller, M. *Delivering Learning on the Net*. London: Kogan Page, 2002.

S. JOSEPH LEVINE is a professor emeritus at Michigan State University.

8

This discussion on assessment and evaluation in the online environment includes the use of different forms of rubrics.

Online Assessment and Evaluation

Stevie Rocco

This chapter focuses on how educators can evaluate and assess individual students in the online environment.

Definition of Terms

This chapter looks at two forms of measurement: those assessing the learner during a lesson and those judging whether a student has met the objectives at the end of the lesson. Defining how these two forms of appraisal will be discussed is important, as individuals often use the terms assessment and evaluation interchangeably.

Here, assessment will refer to activities used to determine the progress of students in meeting lesson or task objectives without regard to grading. This type of formative assessment can range from items as simple as a poll, to a brief questionnaire checking learning, to a focus group based on the progress of the students in meeting objectives midway. Its purpose is to enable the instructor to adjust midstream in order to enable the maximum number of students to meet objectives.

Evaluation will refer to a more formal mode of assessment. Sometimes referred to as summative assessment, this is the basis for judging the skills or knowledge of the students as well as the effectiveness of a unit or activity (New Horizons for Learning, 2002). Generally evaluations form the basis for grading.

NEW DIRECTIONS FOR ADULT AND CONTINUING EDUCATION, no. 113, Spring 2007 © 2007 Wiley Periodicals, Inc.
Published online in Wiley InterScience (www.interscience.wiley.com) • DOI: 10.1002/ace.249

Current Research

When assessment and evaluation are discussed in the literature for online learning, they often focus on the use of online tools for testing (Ko and Rossen, 2004). Quizzes and exams are typically the first resources for instructors who are developing an online course. The reason may be twofold. First, the inclusion of quizzing and testing tools within course management systems may encourage their use. Second, instructors may not have the time or resources available to construct other types of assessments. Interestingly, while much of the literature discusses the technical options available to an instructor in delivering online quizzes and exams, few note the need to align quiz or test questions with course objectives or, indeed, the need to write good questions in the first place (for one exception, see Speck, 2002). This is not to say that technical considerations are unimportant; rather, technical considerations should be weighed in conjunction with a variety of other pedagogical strategies.

In recent years, there has been a shift toward authentic assessment. Authentic assessment attempts to mirror the real-world environment when deciding whether a learner has met the lesson or course objectives. These activities should be "meaningful and valuable" as well as integrated into the learning process (New Horizons for Learning, 2002). Portfolio assessment, problem-based learning, field experiences, and project work can all be considered authentic types of assessment as long as they are aligned with the learning objectives of the instructional unit. The term authentic assessment is most often used in referring to projects or products where evaluation, not assessment of learning in progress, is the focus.

Regarding authentic assessment, Ko and Rossen (2004) state, "The key is planning an adequate variety of activities from which students can assemble a portfolio of their work" (p. 61). Planning a variety of activities is not where authentic assessment and evaluation ends, however. The online instructor must also ensure that the appraisal of these activities is vigorous and reliable.

Methods of Assessment

Assessment is the ability to judge the learning of students in process; that is, it allows the online instructor to see how learners are responding during a lesson and adjust accordingly. Assessment has these qualities:

- Instructor directed. The instructor initiates the assessment.
- Focused on students. The purpose is to improve the teaching-learning process.
- Mutually beneficial to students and instructors. Improvements occur due to feedback.

- Context specific. An assessment for one course may not be appropriate for another.
- Ongoing. It is not sufficient to conduct assessments only the first time a course is offered or even in only one unit of study within a course. Assessment must become integral in order to be most effective (Angelo and Cross, 1993).

In this chapter, two types of assessments are presented: learner-centered methods and content-acquisition methods. Learner-centered methods focus on how students perceive their progress, and content-acquisition methods allow the instructor to see whether students are meeting the objectives according to the instructor's own standards.

Importantly, instructors should ensure that students understand that assessments are not graded. The purpose of assessment is to identify gaps in learning and improve teaching, not to evaluate students. Although instructors might consider giving credit to students for participating, students should not be graded on their responses.

Finally, online instructors should recognize that there is a technical component to assessment in the online environment. Giving students a poll or quizzing them on their understanding requires a technical intermediary for transmission. It is vital that these tools are easy for both students and teachers to use. Instructional designers, technologists, or other support personnel can be helpful in setting up assessments properly.

Learner-Centered Methods. Learner-centered methods can be fairly easy to operationalize in the online environment. These methods ask the students to identify their progress in meeting objectives. In an online course, many questions might be posed to quickly assess how students feel they are doing. For example, in a course in which students study strategic planning, the learners should be able to "identify at least three strategic types." A learner-centered assessment might be a posted survey asking the students to agree or disagree with the following statements:

"I can name the various strategic types studied in this lesson."
"I can give an original example of a differentiation strategy."

Content-Acquisition Methods. Content-acquisition methods can give the instructor direct feedback on whether students are meeting course objectives. Pretests, one such type of assessment, help the instructor to know where to spend more (or less) teaching time.

One method of determining content acquisition during a unit of study is through the use of a single-question survey. The question can relate to one particular objective of a lesson. In the strategic planning course example, if students should be able to "identify at least three strategic types," the instructor might ask the students during a synchronous session to privately identify (using a polling feature or private instant message, for example) what strategy is used by a company that makes expensive dog food for elderly dogs. If students have only a certain amount of time to respond, the instructor can be fairly certain who understands the strategy of differentiation. During an asynchronous threaded discussion, the instructor can ask the students to e-mail him or her one original example of a differentiation strategy.

Content-acquisition assessments are much easier to write for lower-level learning outcomes. This is not to say that content-acquisition assessments of higher-level goals cannot be used, merely that they tend to be more difficult to write and more time-consuming to review.

Methods of Evaluation

Evaluation measures whether students have met lesson or course goals at the end of the unit of study. Below are some common descriptors of evaluation:

- Evaluation is instructor directed.
- Evaluation measures a product rather than a process.
- Evaluation should be predetermined. One of the first elements in preparing an online course is determining what evaluation methods will be used.
- Evaluation is generally graded and can take the form of quizzes, exams, portfolios, field experiences, projects, performances, and papers, among others.
- Evaluation can judge the work of an individual or the work of a team.

Individual Evaluation. An online instructor who decides to evaluate students individually must first determine what type of product will best measure student performance against the objectives. If the objective is simply to be able to identify a series of items, then a selected-response test is appropriate; however, if the student is required to evaluate and then justify a choice, multiple-choice questions will not be sufficient. In that case, an essay exam, performance, or product would align more closely with the desired outcome.

For example, consider a unit in an undergraduate course that contains several knowledge-level objectives and two objectives that require analysis-level thinking. To align the type of evaluation with the objectives, the exam should have multiple-choice or matching and essay questions. Table 8.1 shows the types of questions that can be used with various levels of objectives for a traditional exam.

If an authentic assessment instead of an exam were chosen as a means of evaluation, the instructor would need to decide what type of performance

Table 8.1. Alignment of Objectives with Evaluation for a Traditional Exam

Objective Level	Multiple Choice	True-False	Matching	Completion	Short Answer	Short Essay	Long Essay
Knowledge	X	X	X	X	X		
Comprehension				X	X		
Application				X	X		
Analysis						X	X
Synthesis						X	X
Evaluation						X	X

or product would be most appropriate to the subject and construct an evaluation scheme reflecting the stated objectives. For online instructors who have many students and little time to grade, the careful construction of an evaluation rubric can be the key to increasing student learning while maximizing instructor efficiency.

Group Evaluation. Group evaluation is somewhat more complex because the instructor needs to be sure that the product or performance reflects the knowledge of the entire group and not just one or two members. While Nicolay (2002) suggests that the group receive one evaluation, I prefer to evaluate both the group and the individual (Kagan, 1994). If group tasks are structured such that each individual has particular responsibilities, then there can be individual evaluations based on the parts and a team evaluation based on the whole project.

For example, in an online literature course, students are divided into teams of four and are responsible for creating a Web site on Shakespearean England. Each team member is given responsibility for one aspect of the project: economics, the arts, education, and daily life. Teams report the division of responsibilities to the instructor once they have decided who will be handling each area. The online instructor then creates a second set of teams within the course management system. This second set of teams, or expert groups (Kagan, 1994), works together to compile all the information and data for their aspect of the project. Figure 8.1 shows the breakdown of group membership. Once students have become experts in their area, they return to the project group to integrate their information into the final required format. This structure not only helps to prevent freeloading; it also allows for peer teaching and gives the instructor opportunities for individual and group evaluation.

New Directions for Adult and Continuing Education • DOI: 10.1002/ace

Peer evaluation is another method by which the online instructor can evaluate an entire group. This method is particularly effective when intergroup evaluations are used. For example, if students complete a team project posted online, the instructor can assign each team to evaluate another team's work in a round-robin fashion. Figure 8.2 shows how each team evaluates the production of another team in the class, which then becomes part of that team's evaluation. In the online environment, these evaluations can be administered as surveys using the course management system.

Rubrics are "guides that spell out the criteria for evaluating a task or performance and define levels of quality" (Boston, 2002, p. v). Rubrics are often used for grading (commonly called scoring rubrics), but they can also be used as a tool for assessment (instructional rubrics) as long as the grading component is removed (Andrade, 2005).

Rubrics for Assessment and Evaluation

Here are some general truisms regarding the development and use of rubrics:

- Rubrics should be developed from the objectives for that component.

**Figure 8.1. Project Group and Expert Group Membership
in the Online Environment**

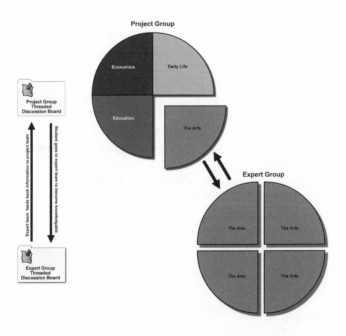

Figure 8.2. Round-Robin Intergroup Peer Evaluation

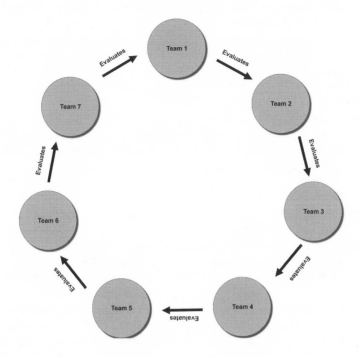

- Rubrics allow teaching to become more efficient.
- Rubrics make requirements more transparent to students.
- If a rubric is to be used for evaluation, students should see it before they complete the assignment.
- Rubrics can give focus to students during any peer review.
- Rubrics give instructors and students a common language to use in determining the extent to which students have met stated objectives.

Many experts assert that there are only two types of rubrics: holistic and analytical (for one example, see Mertler, 2001). To this, I add a third type: primary trait rubrics (Baughin, Brod, and Page, 2002). These are similar to analytical rubrics but are used somewhat differently.

Holistic Rubrics. Holistic rubrics are used to evaluate or assess the whole process, performance, or product. Although holistic rubrics contain criteria, their use is such that the element under investigation is given one score for the entirety of the performance. This type of rubric is predicated on the idea that instructors "know quality when they see it." Using a holistic rubric has these advantages:

- The ability to evaluate a large number of projects quickly

- Transparency in the elements needed for quality for products or assignments where appraisal is thought to be subjective

Holistic rubrics also have some caveats to their use:

- Holistic rubrics require some type of norming process before they are used to ensure consistency of scoring.
- Holistic rubrics should include examples of work that meet every level of the rubric.
- Personality, mood, and other internal elements that can affect grading can be reduced by eliminating student names from projects and evaluating all projects in a single session, as long as the session is not so long that the instructor becomes fatigued.

Disadvantages to using holistic rubrics include the fact that they do not allow variation in the performance: everything is evaluated as all or nothing. Thus, if the student meets one criterion very well but fails to meet another, the result is taken from the lower end, not the average. In Table 8.2, we can see that a student who has difficulty with setting but writes a well-developed plot cannot be evaluated higher than a score of 2.

Analytical Rubrics. These rubrics break a performance or product down into its composite parts. Analytical rubrics consider the parts of the product required to meet objectives and assign weight to each. Table 8.3 is an example of an analytical rubric for an essay. It not only shows the students which elements of the essay are valued, but also which components are the most important—that is, demonstrated understanding is worth more than neat writing.

Table 8.2. Holistic Rubric for a Story

Level	Description
4	The story's plot, characters, and setting were well developed, and the author used sophisticated writing.
3	The plot, characters, and setting were sufficiently developed, and the writing was well developed.
2	The plot, characters, and setting were somewhat developed, but the author did not develop style or tone.
1	The plot, characters, and setting were not sufficiently developed, and detail and organization were lacking.

Table 8.3. Analytic Rubric for an Essay

Requirement The essay...	Score				Score
	1	2	3	4	
Was the required length (between 2 and 10 pages) (2)					10
Contained at least four concrete examples (4)					20
Was clearly written (2)					10
Used appropriate terminology (3)					15
Used a professional tone (3)					15
Demonstrated understanding of the concept (4)					20
Used correct mechanics and usage (2)					10
Was on topic and neatly written (2)					10
Total (20)					100

Note: The requirement weight for each item is in parentheses.

Analytical rubrics:
- Provide considerable information to students who are embarking on an assignment.
- Can be used as a peer review tool to give focus to the reviewer.
- Can be converted from assessment rubrics to evaluation rubrics by adding point values to each component as shown in the last column in Table 8.3.

There are some disadvantages to using this type of rubric:

- Developing an analytical rubric can be a lengthy process.
- Analytical rubrics are rarely perfect the first time they are used.

Primary Trait Rubrics. Primary trait rubrics are similar to analytical rubrics in that they look at a primary trait needed for quality. They can be combined with other types of rubrics (for example, the primary trait of appropriate mechanics in writing could be included in a holistic rubric for a writing assignment). However, primary trait rubrics describe in detail what is required for performance at every level. The participation rubric in Table 8.4 is one example of a primary trait rubric.

Primary trait rubrics are a good place for instructors to begin rubric development for two reasons:

- They force instructors to reflect carefully on all levels of a performance.
- They are modular; if there are common traits used across assignments, each trait can be reused when needed.

Table 8.4. Primary Trait Rubric for Participation in an Online Course

Students are expected to participate in online activities and discussions. Because of the importance of discussion to meeting the objectives of the course, students will be evaluated on the frequency and quality of their participation, including the level of preparation for discussion and student analysis and integration of the assigned materials. Students are expected to communicate their ideas clearly and persuasively. This rubric provides the levels of quality expected in this course.

This level of quality includes all categories below and is distinguishable according to the regular, timely, and high-quality nature of the participation. For example, this level of contribution not only responds to preceding message board postings, but it reflects insight and depth of understanding of course materials and/or stimulates additional relevant discussion.	50 points
This level of quality includes all categories below and includes periodic and timely contributions to class message boards, clear involvement in team exercises, and active, quality responses and questions pertaining to online activities.	40 points
The student regularly logs onto the course system, responds to direct requests for input (for example, e-mail), and contributes to team exercises	30 points
The student irregularly logs on to the course system, fails to reliably respond to requests for input, and does not clearly contribute to team exercises.	Less than 20 points

Source: Adapted from a participation rubric for the Penn State Intercollege MBA. Used with permission.

This type of rubric is also an all-or-nothing type of assessment. The primary trait is the only factor being judged; thus, if several traits are combined, the element with the lowest score in terms of quality determines the overall score.

Table 8.5 shows what happens to the student who uses the synchronous tool creatively but does not demonstrate ease in presenting. That student would earn a score of 2 for the level, because "an ease in manner" is required for a score of 3. Thus, it is important to be careful not to put too many qualities in a primary trait rubric. If more than one trait is needed, then it is probably better to use an analytical rubric made up of those traits instead.

General Guidelines for Developing Rubrics. There are some basic guidelines for instructors who wish to use rubrics in the online environment:

1. Outline your expectations.
2. Divide expectations into traits for a quality performance or product.
3. Decide on a hierarchy of traits.
4. Decide on the rubric format.
5. If you are using a holistic rubric, create sample products for each level of competence.

Table 8.5. Primary Trait Rubric for an Online Presentation, Combining Two Traits

Primary Trait	Level
The presenter was skilled with the tools required for the synchronous presentation and demonstrated an ease in manner, as well as a creative and original use of the tool, which expanded and enhanced the presentation.	4
The presenter was skilled with the tools required for this presentation and demonstrated an ease in manner during the presentation.	3
The presenter was able to use the tools required for this synchronous presentation.	2
The presenter had difficulty using the tools required for this synchronous presentation and was uneasy or nervous during the presentation.	1

6. Share and discuss the rubric with students.
7. Use the rubric.
8. Modify the rubric as needed.

Conclusion

There are many methods available for online instructors wishing to do a good job of assessment and evaluation. From learner-centered methods that allow students to judge their own progress, to content acquisition methods that allow instructors to match progress to objectives, assessment and evaluation methods abound. In fact, these methods are especially important in the online environment because of the lack of face-to-face cues available to instructors to see who is learning the material. The use of rubrics can also enable online instructors to teach more efficiently while improving quality.

References

Andrade, H. G. "Teaching with Rubrics: The Good, the Bad, and the Ugly." *College Teaching*, 2005, 53(1), 27–30.

Angelo, T. A., and Cross, K. P. *Classroom Assessment Techniques.* (2nd ed.) San Francisco: Jossey-Bass, 1993.

Baughin, J. A., Brod, E. F., and Page, D. L. "Primary Trait Analysis: A Tool for Classroom-Based Assessment." *College Teaching*, 2002, 50(2),75–80.

Boston, C. "Introduction." In C. Boston (ed.), *Understanding Scoring Rubrics: A Guide for Teachers.* College Park, Md.: ERIC Clearinghouse on Assessment and Evaluation, 2002.

Kagan, S. *Cooperative Learning.* San Diego, Calif.: Kagan Cooperative Learning, 1994.

Ko, S., and Rossen, S. *Teaching Online: A Practical Guide.* (2nd ed.) Boston: Houghton Mifflin, 2004.

Mertler, C. A. "Designing Scoring Rubrics for Your Classroom." *Practical Assessment, Research and Evaluation,* 2001, 7(25). Retrieved Jan. 15, 2006, from http://pare online.net/.

New Horizons for Learning 2002. *Assessment Terminology: A Glossary of Useful Terms.* 2002. Retrieved Jan. 15, 2006, from http://www.newhorizons.org/strategies/assess/terminology.htm.

Nicolay, J. A. "Group Assessment in the On-Line Learning Environment." In R. S. Anderson, J. F. Bauer, and B. W. Speck (eds.), *Assessment Strategies for the On-Line Class: From Theory to Practice.* San Francisco: Jossey-Bass, 2002.

Speck, B. W. "Learning-Teaching-Assessment Paradigms and the On-Line Classroom." In R. S. Anderson, J. F. Bauer, and B. W. Speck (eds.), *Assessment Strategies for the On-Line Class: From Theory to Practice.* San Francisco: Jossey-Bass, 2002.

STEVIE ROCCO is an instructional designer at Pennsylvania State University.

9

This chapter summarizes and synthesizes the major emphases from the previous chapters, examining their practical implications in online education and suggesting future directions for the practice of adult and continuing education.

Setting Directions for the Future of Online and Adult Education

Simone C. O. Conceição

In 1998, Brad Cahoon edited a volume of New Directions for Adult and Continuing Education titled *Adult Learning and the Internet*. Its focus was the effects of the Internet on adult learning. At that time, use of the Internet was already becoming widespread. Research on online teaching and learning was based on the experiences of instructors who taught online. Such research designs raised issues of reliability and instructional value. However, he said that "as more institutions pursue the development of on-line courses, it becomes increasingly vital that instructors collect and analyze data and share the results of their teaching experiences and peers" (p. 74).

Since the publication of Cahoon's volume, a number of studies on the use of online teaching and learning have emerged. These studies not only include sound research designs but also report reliable and practical results. The chapters in this volume address some of the most recent studies and their applicability in adult and continuing education. In this concluding chapter, I summarize and synthesize the major emphases from the previous chapters, discuss their practical implications, and suggest future directions for adult and continuing education.

NEW DIRECTIONS FOR ADULT AND CONTINUING EDUCATION, no. 113, Spring 2007 © 2007 Wiley Periodicals, Inc.
Published online in Wiley InterScience (www.interscience.wiley.com) • DOI: 10.1002/ace.250

From Planning to Implementation of Online Instruction

Throughout this volume is a focus on the learner, from the planning to the implementation stages of online instruction. Technology is transparent, considered a mere medium for the delivery of online instruction. A common theme for all chapters is the user-driven, learner-centered approach in designing and delivering instruction. Underlying every chapter is the importance of maintaining the pedagogical integrity of the course by ensuring quality user experience.

Chapters One and Two acknowledge the design process for online instruction. Chapter One is particularly concerned with learner characteristics and the role of the instructor. Based on research, online instruction provides evidence of change in the way educators view teaching and learning. This new view requires instructors to rethink the learner's role, the instructor's role, and the design of instruction.

In Chapter Two, Grosjean and Sork contend that converting regular classroom courses into online delivery is not a simple or linear process, and not every instructor is capable of making the transition. The design of online instruction adds concerns to the usual ones of course design. The duration of planning for online instruction can be a long process when involving multiple institutions or programs as part of the collaboration. Modes of delivery may require a consistent look and feel for the learner, showing uniformity in appearance and navigation of the Web environment. Online activities call for active participation of students in discussions by engaging with others on concepts and ideas from the readings. Course evaluation takes a different focus in the online environment. While student evaluations at the end of a traditional course focus on the experience of students with a particular instructor, in the online environment the instructor's role is only one part of a much broader experience. Other aspects should also be taken into consideration when evaluating instruction, such as the technology, the user interface, and the design of content in order to understand the online learner's experience. This means that new methods to evaluate the learner's experience in an online course need to be taken into account.

Teaching Strategies and Implications for Online and Adult Education

Chapters Three to Eight identify six teaching strategies that can be used in the online environment. Each chapter is based on what research reveals about the use of the strategy, a description of the strategy, examples of the use of the teaching strategy in an online course, effectiveness and limitations of the teaching strategy, and implications for practice.

A common premise in these chapters is that online instruction can promote the use of constructivist learning based on the assumption that it can provide the strategies necessary for learners to engage in rich and effective construction of knowledge. Nevertheless, one of the challenges for online instructors is to identify teaching strategies that best fit the needs of learners, content, and the environment. In addition, based on the guiding principles for effective online instruction (Graham and others, 2001), the challenge becomes how to use these guidelines to accomplish effective instruction. One way to overcome these challenges is to identify the instructional and assessment strategies that match the goals and objectives of the course. The instructor may want to consider using multiple teaching strategies to meet diverse learners' needs based on individual or group work, with a focus on content or process.

For online courses that focus on content and process, the use of consensus groups, addressed by Smith and Dirkx in Chapter Three, is ideal because it involves individual work to master a body of knowledge but also involves group work on specific well-defined and well-structured problems and questions. As a constructivist approach to learning, contextualized content encourages active learning, cooperation among learners, time on task, high expectations for learner performance, and creativity and results in increased learner motivation, persistence, and learning outcomes.

Chapter Four by Daley, Cañas, and Stark-Schweitzer presents concept maps: a teaching, learning, and evaluation strategy that can be used in a variety of ways online to facilitate a change in learning and thinking over time. This change in learning and thinking is a more meaningful type of learning because every learner is involved in searching for the relationships between concepts and organizing a structure to the new knowledge that is unique to him or her. From a constructivist perspective, the learner accomplishes this task by linking new information to existing knowledge and experiences. This strategy can be used individually or in groups to analyze concepts and theories in class readings, brainstorm topics for papers, self-reflect on experiences, solve case studies, integrate theory to practice, and evaluate and assess learning. The authors show how CmapTools software provides instructors a way to operationalize the use of concept maps in the online environment and how it can be used to encourage active learning, cooperation, creativity, and instructor feedback through an interactive and dynamic process.

Mentoring as a holistic approach to instruction recognizes learners' needs both within and beyond the content of the online course because it focuses on the long-term development of the learner rather than the short-term performance in the course. Online learners may be in different learning stages of development, have different goals and expectations, and have differing needs from those of their instructors. In Chapter Five, Burgess provides strategies for interacting with novice, marginalized, and underrepresented learners to avoid isolation; keep learners on task; communicate high expectations for learner performance; and provide opportunities to develop their talents through modeling in the online environment.

Learning object repositories may give the impression that they are static, linear, and noninteractive databases that store educational information. On the contrary, depending how they are used, learning object repositories can allow various levels of interactivity and are focused on the learner because they make content easily accessible for learners with diverse and special needs, allow for sharing of information among learners, can be used and reused by learners at their own pace and time, and save the instructor from designing content and spending more time supporting learners. In Chapter Six, Lehman maintains that this teaching strategy promotes cooperation among learners, active learning, time on task, and diverse ways of learning. Although they are in their infancy, learning object repositories have a great potential to facilitate constructivist learning.

Chapter Seven by Levine contends that online discussion boards have the unique capacity to support higher-order constructivist learning and the development of a learning community, an approach that places less emphasis on the instructor and more on the learner. Like many of the other teaching strategies addressed in this volume, discussion boards allow instructors to follow the principles of good online education practice. They support cooperation among learners, active learning, and opportunities for learners to be creative. Levine provides ten conditions to support the effective use of discussion boards.

In Chapter Eight, Rocco discusses assessment strategies that allow instructors to provide individual feedback to learners or have learners assess their own progress in the course. Also addressed in the chapter are evaluation strategies that measure learners' accomplishment of a lesson or course goals at the end of a unit of study. Evaluations may be judged individually or in a group. These strategies, combined with prompt feedback and high expectations guiding principles, make the basis for effective online instruction.

Future Directions for Adult and Continuing Education

Online education is here to stay. This means that adult educators and practitioners need to be aware of the limitations and strengths of this mode of instruction. The chapters in this volume provide evidence that to be effective, online education requires careful planning and facilitation of instruction and change in the way one views teaching and learning. In this process, instructors engage in new kinds of activities that require a different type of connection with learners and the process of teaching through multiple modes of interaction, communication, and exchange.

Some teaching strategies used in the face-to-face environment can be converted to the online environment. They can be successful if individuals are aware of the factors that make online instruction effective. As new technologies such as iPods and Webcasts become more prevalent, instructors must be open and flexible to explore old teaching strategies and experiment with new teaching strategies in order to meet the needs of learners. The online learners of tomorrow will be much more skilled in the use of technologies than the adult learners of today and will demand instruction that meets their needs. As instructors become more comfortable with the new environment, technology will be even more transparent, and experimenting with new teaching strategies will be a natural task for designing instruction. The future of online and adult education holds promise. We must make sure we fulfill that promise.

References

Cahoon, B. "Adult Learning and the Internet: Themes and Things to Come." In B. Cahoon (ed.), *Adult Learning and the Internet*. New Directions for Adult and Continuing Education, no. 78. San Francisco: Jossey-Bass, 1998.

Graham, C., and others. "Seven Principles of Effective Teaching: A Practical Lens for Evaluating Online Courses." *The Technology Source Archives*, Mar./Apr. 2001. Retrieved Oct 14, 2006, from http://technologysource.org/article/seven_principles_of_effective_teaching/.

SIMONE C.O. CONCEIÇÃO is an assistant professor of adult and continuing education at the University of Wisconsin-Milwaukee.

New Directions for Adult and Continuing Education • DOI: 10.1002/ace

INDEX

Back Issue/Subscription Order Form

Copy or detach and send to:

Jossey-Bass, A Wiley Imprint, 989 Market Street, San Francisco, CA 94103-1741

Call or fax toll-free: Phone 888-378-2537 6:30AM – 3PM PST; Fax 888-481-2665

Back Issues: Please send me the following issues at $29 each
(Important: please include series initials and issue number, such as ACE96.)

_____

_____

_____

$ _____ Total for single issues

$ _____ SHIPPING CHARGES: SURFACE   Domestic   Canadian
                                    First Item $5.00 $6.00
                                    Each Add'l Item $3.00 $1.50
                 For next-day and second-day delivery rates, call the number listed above.

Subscriptions: Please __start __renew my subscription to *New Directions for Adult and Continuing Education* for the year 2 _____ at the following rate:

U.S.	__Individual $80	__Institutional $195
Canada	__Individual $80	__Institutional $235
All Others	__Individual $104	__Institutional $269

**For more information about online subscriptions visit
www.interscience.wiley.com**

$ _____ Total single issues and subscriptions (Add appropriate sales tax for your state for single issue orders. No sales tax for U.S. subscriptions. Canadian residents, add GST for subscriptions and single issues.)

__Payment enclosed (U.S. check or money order only)

__VISA __MC __AmEx #_____ Exp. Date _____

Signature _____ Day Phone _____

__ Bill me (U.S. institutional orders only. Purchase order required.)

Purchase order # _____

Federal Tax ID13559302   GST 89102 8052

Name _____

Address _____

_____

Phone _____ E-mail _____

For more information about Jossey-Bass, visit our Web site at www.josseybass.com

OTHER TITLES AVAILABLE IN THE NEW DIRECTIONS FOR
ADULT AND CONTINUING EDUCATION SERIES
Susan Imel, Jovita M. Ross Gordon, COEDITORS-IN-CHIEF

ACE 112 Challenging Homophobia and Heterosexism: lesbian, Gay, Bisexual, and
Queer Issues in Organizational Settings
> *Robert J. Hill*
> This volume is designed for professionals interested in building safe and
> inclusive work and learning environments for adults related to sexual
> orientation, gender identity and gender expression (lesbian, gay, bisexual,
> transgender, and queer people, LGBTQ). Readers will gain knowledge, skills,
> tools, and resources to identify sexual minority needs; cultivate LGBTQ
> networks and ally groups in work settings; dismantle the lavender ceiling
> that prevents sexual minority mobility in organizations; interrogate
> heterosexual privilege and fight homophobia; design and implement
> nonharassment and antidiscrimination policies; achieve domestic partner
> benefits; and build best practices into organizational strategies. It explores
> sexual identity development in the workplace through the lens of
> transformational learning theory and opens new ways to think about career
> development. In addition, this volume offers unique insights into lesbian
> issues in organizations, including the double bind of sexual orientation and
> gender discrimination. Some of the chapter authors look specifically at
> educational settings, such as the continuing professional development of K-
> 12 teachers and the dynamics of dealing with sexual orientation in higher
> education, while others focus on business workplaces. The volume concludes
> with an analysis of public policies and organizational practices that are
> important to LGBTQ lives, with a focus on how organizational policy can
> make space for the emergence of difference related to sexual orientation and
> gender identity.
> ISBN 078799495-2

ACE111 Authenticity in Teaching
> *Patricia Cranton*
> Authenticity is one of those concepts, like soul, spirit, or imagination, that
> are easier to define in terms of what they are not than what they are. We can
> fairly easily say that someone who lies to students or who pretends to know
> things he or she does not know or who deliberately dons a teaching persona
> is not authentic. But do the opposite behaviors guarantee authentic teaching?
> Not necessarily. Becoming an authentic teacher appears to be a
> developmental process that relies on experience, maturity, self-exploration,
> and reflection. It is the purpose of this volume to explore a variety of ways of
> thinking about authenticity in teaching, from the perspective of scholars who
> dedicate themselves to understanding adult education theory and research
> and from that of practitioners who see themselves as working toward
> authentic practice. The contributors address five overlapping and interrelated
> dimensions of authenticity: self-awareness and self-exploration; awareness of
> others (especially students); relationships with students; awareness of
> cultural, social, and educational contexts and their influence on practice; and
> critical self-reflection on teaching.
> ISBN 0-7879-9403-0

ACE110 The Neuroscience of Adult Learning
Sandra Johnson and Kathleen Taylor

Recent research developments have added much to our understanding of brain function. Though some neurobiologists have explored implications for learning, few have focused on learning in adulthood. This issue of New Directions for Adult and Continuing Education, *The Neuroscience of Adult Learning*, examines links between this emerging research and adult educators' practice. Now that it is possible to trace the pathways of the brain involved in various learning tasks, we can also explore which learning environments are likely to be most effective. Volume contributors include neurobiologists, educators, and clinical psychologists who have illuminated connections between how the brain functions and how to enhance learning. Among the topics explored here are basic brain architecture and "executive" functions of the brain, how learning can "repair" the effects of psychological trauma on the brain, effects of stress and emotions on learning, the centrality of experience to learning and construction of knowledge, the mentor-learner relationship, and intersections between best practices in adult learning and current neurobiological discoveries. Although the immediate goal of this volume is to expand the discourse on teaching and learning practices, our overarching goal is to encourage adult learners toward more complex ways of knowing.
ISBN 0-7879-8704-2

ACE109 Teaching for Change: Fostering Transformative Learning in the Classroom
Edward W. Taylor

Fostering transformative learning is about teaching for change. It is not an approach to be taken lightly, arbitrarily, or without much thought. Many would argue that it requires intentional action, a willingness to take personal risk, a genuine concern for the learners' betterment, and the wherewithal to draw on a variety of methods and techniques that help create a classroom environment that encourages and supports personal growth. What makes the work of transformative learning even more difficult is the lack of clear signposts or guidelines that teachers can follow when they try to teach for change. There is now a need to return to the classroom and look through the lens of those who have been engaged in the practice of fostering transformative learning. This volume's authors are seasoned practitioners and scholars who have grappled with the fundamental issues associated with teaching for change (emotion, expressive ways of knowing, power, cultural difference, context, teacher authenticity, spirituality) in a formal classroom setting; introduced innovations that enhance the practice of fostering transformative learning; and asked ethical questions that need to be explored and reflected upon when practicing transformative learning in the classroom.
ISBN 0-7879-8584-8

ACE108 Adulthood: New Terrain
Mary Alice Wolf

One of the many surprises about the lifespan perspective is that individuals, families, institutions, and corporations lead *many* lives. The purpose of this resource is to acquaint and update practitioners in adult education and related roles with emerging and creative methods of 1) appreciating the learner's perspective, 2) moderating content and learning format to enhance

meaning-making in the learning environment, and 3) developing tools to address alternative modes of development and growth that occur in adult-hood and challenge adult educators on a daily basis. What does the new adult learner look like? This volume contains theory and research on learners who turn to educational programs in times of transition and explores ways of connecting with new cognitive and affective meanings. This volume explores dimensions of adult development from ethnographic, research, and theoretical perspectives. It addresses adult learners' experience and meaning of education as an ongoing resource for well-being and positive development across the lifecourse. It updates the reader in the emerging terrain of adult-hood; adult learning philosophies are implemented and modified to meet adults' developmental mandate to continue learning in order to make meaning and find purpose during the countless transitions of the ever-increasing adult years.
ISBN 0-7879-8396-0

ACE107 **Artistic Ways of Knowing: Expanded Opportunities for Teaching and Learning**
Randee Lipson Lawrence
This volume of *New Directions for Adult and Continuing Education* challenges the dominant paradigm of how knowledge is typically constructed and shared in adult education settings by focusing on ways in which adult educators can expand learning opportunities and experiences for their learners. Art appeals universally to us all and has the capacity to bridge cultural differences. Art can also foster individual and social transformation, promoting dialogue and deepening awareness of ourselves and the world around us. The contributors to this volume include actors, musicians, photographers, storytellers, and poets, all of whom also happen to be adult educators. In each chapter, the author describes how one or more forms of artistic expression were used to promote learning in formal or informal adult education settings. In each case, the purp-ose of education was not to teach art (that is, not to develop expertise in acting, poetry writing, or creating great works of art). Conversely, art was used as a means to access learning in subjects as divergent as English language acquisition, action research, community awareness, and social justice.
ISBN 0-7879-8284-9

ACE106 **Class Concerns: Adult Education and Social Class**
Tom Nesbitt
This volume of *New Directions for Adult and Continuing Education* brings together several leading progressive adult educators to explore how class affects different arenas of adult education practice and discourse. It high- lights the links between adult education, the material and social conditions of daily and working lives, and the economic and political systems that under-pin them. Chapters focus on adult education policies; teaching; learning and identity formation; educational institutions and social movements; and the relationships between class, gender, and race. Overall, the volume reaffirms the salience of class in shaping the lives we lead and the educational approaches we develop. It offers suggestions for adult educators to identify and resist the encroachments of global capitalism and understand the role of education in promoting social equality. Finally, it suggests that a class perspective can provide an antidote to much of the social amnesia, self-absorption, and apolitical theorizing that pervades current adult education discourse.
ISBN 0-7879-8128-1

ACE105 HIV/AIDS Education for Adults
John P. Egan
Contributors from the United States, Canada, and Australia, working in university-based and community-based environments and for divergent communities—present specific experiences in the fight against HIV/AIDS. They share stories of shifting paradigms and challenging norms, and of seeking and finding innovation. Topics examined include the struggle for meaning and power in HIV/AIDS education, HIV prevention workers and injection drug users, community-based research, grassroots response to HIV/AIDS in Nova Scotia, sex workers and HIV/AIDS education, and the Tuskegee Syphilis Study and legacy recruitment for experimental vaccines. By examining HIV/AIDS through an adult education lens, we gain insights into how communities (and governments) can respond quickly and effectively to emergent health issues—and other issues linked to marginalization.
ISBN 0-7879-8032-3

ACE104 Embracing and Enhancing the Margins of Adult Education
Meg Wise, Michelle Glowacki-Dudka
Adult educators increasingly risk and resist being placed at the margins of academic and other organizations. This volume argues that depending on how those margins are defined, margins can be a place of creativity and power from which to examine and challenge dominant ideology and practice. Chapters explore advances and effective practices being made in the margins of adult education from several perspectives including community-based programs, interreligious learning, human resource development, African American underrepresentation in the academy, and degree granting adult education programs. Other areas explored include an interdisciplinary Web-based patient education research program and educational focus on citizenship and public responsibility skills.
ISBN 0-7879-7859-0

ACE103 Developing and Delivering Adult Degree Programs
James P. Pappas, Jerry Jerman
The explosive growth in adult degree programs is fueled by increased distance education technologies, potential for providing additional revenue streams for institutions, fierce competition from the private sector and from other higher education institutions, and rising interest in interdisciplinary programs. This issue explores adult degree programs and considers the theoretical under-pinnings of such programs and hands-on issues as curriculum, faculty, marketing, technology, financing, and accreditation, all with a goal of informing and equipping both scholars and practitioners.
ISBN 0-7879-7767-5

ACE102 Promoting Critical Practice in Adult Education
Ralf St. Clair, Jennifer A. Sandlin
The idea that critical perspectives on teaching are difficult to enact in the classrooms is not new. And what do we mean by *critical perspectives* anyway? In this volume some of the most exciting scholars in adult education—whether established or emerging—provide insights into what it means to be critical and how it affects the concrete practices of teaching adults. Chapter topics include critical theory, feminism, critical postmodernism, Africentrism, queer theory, and cultural studies.
ISBN 0-7879-7590-7